A Broadcast Engineering Tutorial
for Non-Engineers

THIRD EDITION

A Broadcast Engineering Tutorial for Non-Engineers

THIRD EDITION

Graham Jones
National Association of Broadcasters

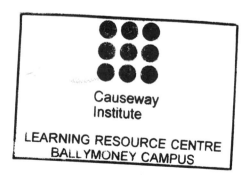

AMSTERDAM • BOSTON • HEIDELBERG
LONDON • NEW YORK • OXFORD • PARIS
SAN DIEGO • SAN FRANCISCO • SINGAPORE
SYDNEY • TOKYO

ELSEVIER

Focal Press is an imprint of Elsevier

Acquisition Editor: Angelina Ward
Project Manager: Kyle Sarofeen
Assistant Editor: Becky Golden-Harrell
Marketing Manager: Christine Degon
Cover Design: Eric DeCicco

Focal Press is an imprint of Elsevier
30 Corporate Drive, Suite 400, Burlington, MA 01803, USA
Linacre House, Jordan Hill, Oxford OX2 8DP, UK

∞ Recognizing the importance of preserving what has been written, Elsevier prints its books
on acid-free paper whenever possible.

Library of Congress Cataloging-in-Publication Data
Jones, Graham.
  A broadcast engineering tutorial for non-engineers / Graham Jones.—3rd
ed
     p. cm.
  Includes index.
  ISBN-13: 978-0-240-80700-3   ISBN-10: 0-240-80700-6
  1. Radio—Transmitters and transmission.   2. Television—Transmitters and
transmission.   3. Radio broadcasting.   4. Television broadcasting.   I.
Title.
  TK6561.J66 2005
  621.384—dc22

                                        2005006432

British Library Cataloguing-in-Publication Data
A catalogue record for this book is available from the British Library.

ISBN-13: 978-0-240-80700-3
ISBN-10: 0-240-80700-6

For information on all Focal Press publications
visit our website at www.books.elsevier.com

05 06 07 08 09 10   10 9 8 7 6 5 4 3 2

Printed in the United States of America

Working together to grow
libraries in developing countries

www.elsevier.com | www.bookaid.org | www.sabre.org

ELSEVIER   **BOOK AID**
              International   Sabre Foundation

Contents

Preface

There are many people without engineering backgrounds who need to have a general understanding of broadcast engineering principles. They may be broadcast managers, program producers, or other professionals who deal with broadcast clients. This tutorial is intended to help non-engineers who want to learn something about the technicalities of radio and television. It should also be useful for engineers in training, or those in technical occupations who want an overview of areas outside their area of expertise. We explain the jargon of broadcasting and describe the underlying principles, standards, and equipment for broadcast facilities, in terms a layperson can understand.

The third edition has been completely revised to reflect the increasing use of digital techniques in all aspects of television and radio broadcasting. It has been reorganized and some obsolete material removed, while also updating the basic information on traditional analog technologies. New chapters have been added to provide an overview of first principles and current standards in the broadcast industry. We concentrate on over-the-air broadcasting from U.S. radio and television stations, but also mention some of the other methods of program delivery to the home and outline some of the different standards and technologies used in other countries.

Although later chapters build on information in earlier sections, this book can be consulted for information about a particular topic. We hope that the information in these pages will help readers further their understanding of our trade, and thus enhance their ability to perform the broadcast-related functions of their jobs.

NAB Science and Technology Department

Acknowledgments

As the principal author and editor of the third edition of this tutorial, I would like to acknowledge the contributions I have received in preparing the book. The foundation, of course, was the second edition, which came from NAB Science and Technology, although very little of that work remains unchanged. I have received advice and support from my colleagues at NAB: Art Allison, Janet Elliott, David Layer, John Marino, and Kelly Williams, and from the Senior Vice President of Science and Technology, Lynn Claudy. James Snyder provided input on Internet broadcasting and advised on several other topics, as did Ed Williams. Advice on information technology came from Andrew Jones and John Roberts. Finally, thanks to my wife, Linda, for putting up with the long hours spent in putting this work together and for being the ultimate "non-engineer" who had to understand everything in the book.

Graham Jones
Washington, D.C.

CHAPTER 1

Introduction

In its simplest form, a radio or television broadcast station consists of two basic facilities: the studio complex and a transmitter site. The studio complex is the place where the programming originates. The transmitter is the device that, with an antenna, actually broadcasts the program material out over the air. In between the two is a connection called the studio transmitter link. In reality, there are many components that make up the chain from program origination through to the final viewer or listener. This tutorial provides an introduction to the technologies and equipment that constitute modern broadcasting systems.

Traditionally, broadcasting was based on *analog* techniques, but for more than 20 years there has been a steady migration to *digital* systems, which provide many benefits for studio operations. The increasing use of computer-based information technology has revolutionized both radio and television studios. More recently, new standards have evolved that now allow digital transmission to the home for both radio and television.

All types of broadcast stations used for domestic broadcasting (AM, FM, and TV) are covered in this tutorial, with descriptions of both analog and digital studio and transmission systems where appropriate. For completeness, satellite, cable, and Internet delivery are also briefly mentioned.

Jargon words and phrases are shown in *italics* the first time they are used in each section. They may be explained there or covered in detail in other chapters. Some of these jargon words are unique to broadcasting, but some are regular words that are used in a special way—we will try to make their meaning clear for the reader.

Chapters in the first section of the book, Broadcasting Basics, discuss the main methods used for radio and television broadcasting and explain some of the basic science and the terms used later in the book. Chapters in the second section, Studios and Production Facilities, describe radio and television studios and remote operations, covering the main items of equipment used and how they work together. Chapters in the third section, Transmission Standards and Systems, discuss the standards and technologies used for U.S. radio and television transmission, and cover transmitter site facilities and equipment. The final chapter discusses radio wave propagation and the Federal Communications Commission (FCC) Technical Rules.

In each section or chapter, we generally talk about topics related to audio and radio first, and then deal with video and television.

BROADCASTING BASICS

CHAPTER 2

Types of Broadcasting

By definition, broadcasting means "to transmit by radio or television," but, with developments in technology that have taken place, that simple phrase now includes many different types of transmission. Let's start with a summary of the main types in use today in the United States and overseas. Many of the systems mentioned below differ only in the way they are transmitted—studio systems for radio and television generally have fewer variations. Don't worry if you don't fully understand all of the terms used in this chapter: they will be explained later in the appropriate sections.

Analog Radio

Radio broadcasting for local stations in the United States, and throughout the world falls into two main types: AM and FM—standing for *amplitude modulation* and *frequency modulation*, respectively. These are the particular methods of radio transmission, used for many years for traditional broadcasting to home, car, and portable receivers. In North America, AM is used in the *medium frequency* (MF) (also known as *medium wave)* band, whereas FM uses the *very high frequency* (VHF) band.

One radio station frequently feeds only one transmitter, and therefore is referred to as an AM station or an FM station. It is, however, quite possible for a station to feed both AM and FM transmitters in the same area, or to feed more than one transmitter covering different areas, in which case the term AM or FM may refer only to a particular transmitter and not to the station as a whole.

In some overseas countries, AM is also used in the *long wave* band, with frequencies somewhat lower than the MF band, and slightly different propagation characteristics—good for broadcasting over a wide area. AM is also used for *shortwave* radio broadcasting—also known as HF from the name of the *high frequency* band that is used. This is used for broadcasting over very long distances (usually internationally).

We cover analog radio in more detail in Chapters 12 and 16.

Digital Radio

There are four main over-the-air digital radio systems in the world, all different from each other in several respects: IBOC, DAB, ISDB-TSB, and DRM.

IBOC

Digital radio broadcasting for local stations in the United States, introduced for regular use in 2003, uses a proprietary system called HD Radio, generically known as IBOC. IBOC stands for In-Band On-Channel and is the particular method of digital radio transmission. There are two versions: one for AM broadcasting and one for FM. They offer significant quality improvements over equivalent analog AM and FM transmission, while broadcasting to the same destinations of home, car, and portable receivers. FM IBOC can also carry additional data information services. A key feature of IBOC is that it can share the same band and channel as an analog radio transmitter (hence, the name), so no additional radio spectrum space is needed for a radio station to add an IBOC digital service.

We cover IBOC in more detail in Chapters 13 and 16.

DAB

Digital radio for national and some local services outside the United States—in Europe, Canada, and elsewhere—primarily uses a system called DAB. First introduced in the United Kingdom in 1995, DAB stands for Digital Audio Broadcasting, which is also known as Eureka 147 and, in the United Kingdom, as Digital Radio. DAB has quality advantages similar to FM IBOC but is fundamentally different in that it is intended for multiprogramming network services. Unlike IBOC, it cannot share a channel with an analog broadcast. Each DAB transmission requires much more RF spectrum since it contains multiple program services (typically six to eight, depending on quality and the amount of data carried). This makes it impractical for use by a single radio station. DAB can only be used where suitable frequency bands are available, with channel capacity not allocated to other services. In Europe, it is currently being transmitted using frequencies in the VHF band, and in Canada in the *L-Band* (see explanation of Frequencies, Bands, and Channels in Chapter 4). These bands are fully allocated for other purposes in the United States, including broadcasting, land mobile, and military communications.

ISDB-TSB

ISDB-TSB stands for Integrated Services Digital Broadcasting–Terrestrial Sound Broadcasting and is the digital radio system developed for Japan, where the first services started in 2003. Like DAB, ISDB-TSB is intended for multiprogram services, and is currently using transmission frequencies in the VHF band. One unique feature of this system is that the digital radio channels are intermingled with ISDB digital television channels in the same band.

DRM

DRM stands for Digital Radio Mondiale, a system developed primarily as a direct replacement for AM international broadcasting in the *shortwave* band, although DRM can also be used in the medium wave and long wave bands. DRM uses the same channel plan as the analog services, and, with some restrictions and changes to the analog service, a DRM broadcast can possibly share the same channel with an analog station. DRM is a mono (single audio channel) system when used with existing channel allocations, but stereo (two-channel) audio may be possible in the future if wider channels are available. DRM started trial implementations in several countries in 2003.

Satellite Radio

XM and Sirius

There are two similar but competing satellite radio services in the United States: XM Satellite Radio and Sirius Satellite Radio, both licensed as Satellite Digital Audio Radio Services (SDARS). XM and Sirius are subscription services, and each broadcasts more than 100 digital audio channels, intended primarily for reception by car, portable, and fixed receivers. XM uses two high-power *geostationary* satellites (their location in the sky does not change relative to the earth's surface) that transmit with frequencies in the *S-Band* (see explanation of Frequencies, Bands, and Channels in Chapter 4). This provides coverage of the complete continental United States and parts of Canada and Mexico. Sirius is similar except that it uses three nonstationary satellites, with more coverage of Canada and Mexico than XM. Both systems use ground-based *repeaters* to fill in many of the gaps where the satellite signals may be blocked.

WorldSpace

WorldSpace Satellite Radio is an international satellite radio service that broadcasts more than 100 digital audio channels, some by subscription and some free of charge, to many countries around the world. There are currently two geostationary satellites covering Africa, the Middle East, most of Asia, and much of Europe. A third satellite is planned for South America, with a fourth for further coverage in Europe. Some WorldSpace channels are also carried on XM Radio in the United States. Transmissions are intended for reception by portable and fixed receivers, using frequencies in the *L-Band*.

Analog Television

NTSC

In North America, Japan, and some other countries, television has been broadcast for many years using the NTSC system. NTSC stands for National Television System Committee, which developed the original standard. The standard defines the format of the *video* that carries the picture information, and also how the video and audio signals are transmitted. NTSC is broadcast over the air on channels in the VHF and *ultra high frequency* (UHF) bands. NTSC television can also be carried on analog cable and satellite delivery systems. In the United States, NTSC is now being phased out and replaced by ATSC digital television, with an eventual end of analog transmissions.

PAL and SECAM

Many countries in Europe, Australia, and other parts of the world use a color television system called PAL. The underlying technologies used are the same as NTSC, but the color coding and picture structure is different. PAL stands for Phase Alternating Line, which refers to the way the color information is carried on alternating lines. SECAM is another color television system used for transmission in France, Russia, and a few other countries. SECAM stands for the French words Sequential Couleur avec Mémoire, which refer to the way the color information is sent sequentially and stored from one line to the next. PAL television signals are transmitted in a similar way to NTSC, but the size of the RF channel is different; the SECAM transmission system has several differences from both NTSC and PAL.

We cover PAL and SECAM in more detail in Chapter 5, and NTSC in more detail in Chapters 5, 14, and 16.

Digital Television

Over-the-air digital television, DTV, is also referred to as Digital Terrestrial Television Broadcasting or DTTB. There are three main DTV systems in the world, all with significant differences: ATSC, DVB-T, and ISDB-T. China is in the process of developing its own system but, at the time of writing this book, details have not yet been finalized.

ATSC

ATSC stands for Advanced Television Systems Committee and is the DTV standard for the United States, where DTV broadcasting started in 1996. ATSC has also been adopted by Canada, Mexico, and Korea, and is being considered by some other countries. The ATSC system allows transmission of both *standard definition* (SD) and *high definition* (HD or HDTV) program services, with capabilities including widescreen 16:9 *aspect ratio* pictures, *surround sound* audio, *electronic program guide*, *multicasting*, and *datacasting*. ATSC DTV is transmitted over the air in the same VHF and UHF bands as NTSC television, using vacant channels in the NTSC channel allocation plan for the country. Cable television systems also carry DTV programs produced for ATSC transmission, but do not actually use the transmission part of the ATSC standard.

We cover ATSC in more detail in Chapters 6, 15, and 16.

DVB-T

Terrestrial DTV in Europe, Australia, and many other countries uses the DVB-T standard, which stands for Digital Video Broadcasting–Terrestrial. DVB-T allows transmission of both SD and HD programs, and most of its capabilities are generally similar to ATSC. The particular picture formats used, however, are usually based on the analog television system used in the relevant country. Currently, most countries using DVB-T, apart from Australia, do not transmit in high definition, but Europe is now considering the possibility of adding HD services.

Like ATSC, DVB-T is transmitted over the air in the VHF and UHF television bands. The main difference from ATSC, apart from the picture formats used, is in the method of transmission. ATSC uses a modulation system called 8-VSB, whereas DVB-T uses COFDM with QAM or QPSK modulation (all of these terms are explained in later chapters). As in the United States, DVB-T services will eventually replace analog television broadcasting.

ISDB-T

Japan uses ISDB-T, the Integrated Services Digital Broadcasting–Terrestrial standard, to broadcast both SD and HD programs in the VHF and UHF television bands. Modulation and other transmission arrangements have some similarities to DVB-T, but the system uses *data segments* in the transmitted signal to provide more flexible multiprogram arrangements for different services and reception conditions. ISDB-T will eventually replace analog broadcasting.

Satellite Television

Medium- and Low-Power Services

Many television services are distributed in the United States and elsewhere using medium- and low-power geostationary satellites in the C and Ku-Bands (explained in Chapter 4), some with analog and some with digital transmissions. Although many of these are intended for professional users (e.g., distribution to cable television headends or to broadcast stations), some can be received by consumers using large satellite dishes, typically 6 to 10 feet in diameter. These are sometimes known as "big ugly dishes" (BUDs). Some channels are transmitted *in the clear* and are free of charge, whereas others are *encrypted* and require a subscription to allow them to be viewed. Many network feeds are carried but very few individual broadcast stations have their programs distributed in this way.

Digital Satellite Broadcasting

In the United States, direct broadcasting by satellite (DBS) digital television services to the home, also known as direct to home (DTH), are provided by several operators (at this time, the main ones are DirecTV and Dish Network). They use a small number of high-power geostationary satellites to provide several hundred subscription channels, including both SD and HD, and carry many local broadcast station channels. These DBS services use transmissions in the Ku-Band that can be received over most of the United States with a small 18 to 24 inch diameter dish.

There are numerous DBS service providers in other parts of the world. Key features are the capability to cover very large areas— many countries or even a continent—from one satellite, generally with capacity for large numbers of program channels. Services in Europe and some other countries use the DVB-S (Digital Video Broadcasting–Satellite) standard, and Japan uses ISDB-S (Integrated Services Digital Broadcasting–Satellite).

In Japan, some analog television services have been transmitted using high-power satellites. These services are being phased out in favor of digital DBS.

Cable Television

Cable television systems provided by multiple service operators (MSOs) distribute large numbers of television and audio program channels over networks of cables spanning urban and suburban areas. They do not usually cover large rural areas due to the greater distances between homes. Such services carry a subscription fee and always carry program services from all or most of the broadcast stations in the area, as well as numerous other channels.

Analog Cable

Traditional analog cable carries television channels at *radio frequency* (RF) on one or two cables connected into the home, using similar bands as over-the-air broadcast television, but with slightly different channels and a wider range of frequencies. In the United States, apart from the channel allocations, the cable television signal is basically identical to NTSC broadcast over-the-air.

Digital Cable

Digital cable services can be carried on the same cable as analog, using different channel allocations for the analog and digital signals. In the United States, digital cable may carry SD and HD DTV programs produced for ATSC transmission, but the modulation system used is *quadrature amplitude modulation* (QAM), which is different from the over-the-air standard. Both DVB and ISDB have digital cable variants of their DTV standards. Services in Europe and some other countries use the DVB-C (Digital Video Broadcasting–Cable) standard, and Japan uses ISDB-C (Integrated Services Digital Broadcasting–Cable).

Groups and Networks

Terrestrial Broadcasting

Most large towns in the United States have at least one or two local AM or FM radio stations and one or more television stations. Large cities usually have many more. Some of these stations are individually owned, but many belong to station groups that also own other stations, in some cases many hundreds. Some stations, known as "O and Os" (owned and operated), are owned by the broadcast networks themselves.

The major television networks in the United States are ABC, CBS, Fox, NBC, and the Public Broadcasting Service, but there are others. The major radio networks are ABC Radio, American Urban Radio, AP Radio, CBS, Jones Radio, UPI Radio, USA Radio, Westwood One, and the public broadcasting National Public Radio and Public Radio International, but there are many others. Networks produce programs, often including news services, for distribution to stations that they own and to other stations in the network, known as *affiliates*. Local radio and TV stations may produce some of their own programming, especially local news and weather, which is slotted in between the network programming. Commercial stations sell their own advertising time, with locally originated advertisements, transmitted in addition to any network-originated advertising they are required to carry.

Some station group owners may produce or originate programming (particularly news-type programs) at a central location and distribute it to their individual stations at remote locations. This arrangement is known as *centralcasting*.

Cable and Satellite

The term network is also often used to describe companies that produce one or more programs for distribution to multiple cable and satellite operators, but not to terrestrial broadcast stations. Examples of cable and satellite networks are CNN (Cable News Network) and HBO (Home Box Office); there are many others.

Internet Radio and Television

With the rise of the Internet in the 1990s, a new distribution medium for radio and television programming developed. *Streaming* technologies make possible the distribution of audio and video over the Internet. Unlike broadcasting, the programming is available only to those with access to the Internet using compatible computer equipment and software.

Service Implications

How and whether broadcasters decide to provide streaming services to Internet customers requires many decisions. Rights management, copyright payments, and control of distribution of copyrighted material are all major factors in what programs and advertisements can be made available to consumers and how much they must pay to use them. However, it is clear that distribution of streaming audio and video media via the Internet is now a major force in program distribution. It can serve as an alternative distribution medium, provide a value-added service that may add revenue from a given program, and allow distribution beyond traditional borders to the entire world. See Chapter 7 for more details on this topic.

CHAPTER 3
Sound and Vision

This chapter describes some of the scientific principles that are fundamental to all types of broadcasting. It covers the physical properties of light and sound, and how the basic workings of human hearing and vision allow us to perceive sound from audio signals and moving color images from video signals. We will build on these principles later in the book, when we discuss how studio and transmission equipment and systems work.

Sound and Audio

Sound Waves

As you probably already know, the sounds that we hear are actually pressure waves in the air, which cause our eardrums to vibrate. Everything that produces a sound, whether a guitar string, a jet airplane, a human voice, or a loudspeaker, does so by causing a vibration that sets off the pressure wave.

Sound waves are an example of an *analog* signal—they have continuous, and generally smooth, variations—and the loudness and pitch of the sound that we hear are directly proportional to the variations in pressure in the air. The *amplitude* of the pressure wave determines how loud it sounds, and the *frequency* determines whether it sounds high or low in tone. Low notes (bass) have low frequencies and high notes (treble) have high frequencies. Frequency is measured in *cycles per second*, and this unit is usually known as a *hertz* or Hz. The highest frequency that most people can hear is between 15 and 20 thousand hertz (kHz), although the high range is reduced for most people as they get older. Frequencies below about 30 Hz are felt rather than heard.

A pure single tone has a single frequency, known as a *sine wave*. Figure 3.1 illustrates this graphically, as a plot of sound pressure level against time. More complex sounds are made up from many individual sine waves of different frequencies and amplitudes, all added together. The mixture of different sine waves determines the shape of the wave and the character of the sound we hear.

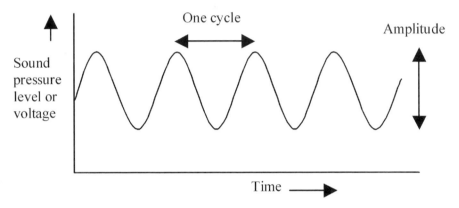

Figure 3.1. Analog Audio Sine Wave

Audio

Most people have some idea of what *microphones* and *loudspeakers* are for. A microphone turns a sound pressure wave in the air into an electrical audio *signal* that matches the amplitude of the pressure wave. In the reverse process, a loudspeaker receives the electrical audio signal and turns it back into sound waves in the air that we can hear. Figure 3.1 also illustrates the electrical audio *waveform* for a sine wave, as well as the pressure wave. This audio signal is a varying *voltage* (the unit of "pressure" for electricity) that can be recorded and processed in many ways, and ultimately transmitted over-the-air—as discussed later in the book.

The range of frequencies in an audio signal, ranging from the lowest to the highest frequency carried, is known as the *bandwidth* of the signal. The range of frequencies that can be passed, combined with information on how accurately their amplitudes are reproduced, is known as the *frequency response* of the equipment or system.

With analog audio, the electrical signal is a direct equivalent of the sound pressure wave that it represents. However, it is possible for an analog signal to lose some of its frequencies or to have *distortion* and *noise* added to it as it passes through the *signal chain* from source to listener. Losing high or low frequencies makes the sound lacking in treble or bass; distortion makes the sound harsh and unpleasant, and noise of various sorts makes it more difficult to hear the original sound clearly. Therefore, analog audio is often converted to more robust digital signals for processing and transmission, with many advantages, as described later.

Mono, Stereo, and Surround Sound

Sounds picked up with a single microphone can be carried through a signal chain as a single channel, and end up being played to a listener on a single loudspeaker. Such a source and system is known as *monophonic* or *mono*. The drawback of mono audio is that it does not provide the listener with any real sense of direction or space for the sounds. If the sounds are picked up with two or more microphones, carried to the listener over two separate channels, and played over two loudspeakers, left and right, then it is possible to provide a good impression of the position of the sound in the original studio. Such a system is known as *stereophonic* or *stereo*, and is widely used in audio recording, radio, and television.

Stereo systems are, however, unable to give an impression of the direction of sounds coming from the sides or behind the listener, or to give a proper impression of the acoustics of the space. This can be achieved by using multiple, properly positioned microphones, a multichannel signal chain, and multiple loudspeakers positioned in front of and around the listener. This is known as a *surround sound* system.

Light and Video

Light and Color

We have learned that sound is a vibration, generated by the source of sound, that produces a pressure wave, which makes the eardrum vibrate, and so we hear the sound. In a similar manner, light is a type of wave (an *electromagnetic wave*) that is generated by the source of light, which stimulates the retina in the eye so we can see it. Just as the amplitude of the sound wave determines the loudness of the sound, the amplitude of the light wave determines the brightness of the light, which is referred to as the *luminance* level. The frequency of the sound wave determines whether we hear a low or a high tone, and similarly for light, the frequency of the wave determines what color we see, referred to as its *hue*. One other characteristic of colored light is its *saturation*. Saturation refers to how "strong" the color is, or, to put it another way, how much it has been diluted with white light. For example, a deep bright red is very saturated, whereas a light pink may have the same hue, but with a low saturation.

What we see as white light is, in fact, made up of a mixture of many colors that the brain interprets as being white. This can be demonstrated by shining a white light through a glass prism, which splits up the different colors so they can be seen individually. That also happens when we see a rainbow. In that case, each raindrop acts as a tiny prism, and the white sunlight is split up into all the colors of the rainbow. What is perhaps more surprising is that the same sensation of white light in the eye can be produced by mixing together just three colors in the right proportion. For light mixing, these *primary colors* are red, green, and blue, also referred to as R, G, and B.

By mixing two of these colors together, we can produce other *secondary colors*, so:

> Red + Green = Yellow
> Red + Blue = Magenta
> Green + Blue = Cyan

By mixing the primary colors in different proportions, we can actually produce most other visible colors. This important property means that the light from any color scene can be split up, using *color filters* or a special sort of prism, into just the three primary colors of red, green, and blue, for converting into television pictures.

Characteristics of the Human Eye

We mentioned previously that the retina in the eye is stimulated by light, and we then see the scene. The human eye and brain perceive different light frequencies as different colors. Several other characteristics of human vision are significant in this process. One of these is that the eye sees much less color detail compared to the detail it sees in the brightness, or luminance, of a scene. This greatly affects the way that color signals are carried in color television systems (see the sections on chrominance in Chapter 5 and color subsampling in Chapter 6). Another characteristic is called *persistence of vision*. After an image being viewed has disappeared, the eye still sees the image for a fraction of a second (just how long depends on the brightness of the image). This allows a series of still pictures in both television and cinematography to create the illusion of a continuous moving picture.

Video

Most people have some idea of what television *cameras* and television *receivers* or *picture monitors* are used for. In summary, a color camera turns the light that it receives into an electrical video signal for each of the three primary red, green, and blue colors. In the reverse process, a television display or picture monitor receives the electrical video signal and turns it back into red green, and blue light that we can see. Our eyes combine the red, green, and blue images together so we see the full color scene. The video signal that carries the image is a varying voltage, and that signal can be recorded and processed in many ways and transmitted over-the air—as covered later in this book.

With analog video, the electrical video signal is a direct equivalent of the luminance of the light that it represents (and in a more complicated way, also of the color hue and saturation). However, it is possible for an analog signal to have distortion and noise added to it as it passes through the *signal chain* from source to viewer. Different types of distortion change the picture in many ways, making it soft and fuzzy, adding a "ghost" image, or changing the colors. Video noise may be seen as "snow" or random spots or patterns on the screen. Therefore, analog video is often converted to more robust digital signals for processing and transmission, with many advantages, as described in later chapters.

Baseband

The audio and video signals we have mentioned, directly representing sound and image information, are referred to as *baseband* signals. They can be carried as varying voltages over wires and cables and can be processed by various types of equipment. They cannot, however, be transmitted over-the-air by themselves. For that they need to be combined in a special way, called *modulation*, with radio frequency signals, as discussed in the next chapter.

CHAPTER 4

Radio Frequency Waves

This chapter describes some of the scientific principles of radio waves that are fundamental to all types of broadcasting transmission.

Electromagnetic Waves

It is fairly easy to understand that sound waves can be carried through the air, just as waves move on the sea. Although more difficult to explain, as mentioned earlier, light can also be considered as an *electromagnetic wave*. In simple terms, electromagnetic waves are vibrations of electrical and magnetic energy that can travel long distances, even through the vacuum of space or, to a variable extent, through other materials. They are the foundation of broadcasting.

Types of Waves

Electromagnetic waves have a range of frequencies, most of them far higher than the sound waves described previously. The waves have very different properties, depending on the frequency, and the following types make up the electromagnetic radiation *spectrum*. Starting from the lowest frequencies, they are as follows:

- Radio waves
- Microwaves (very short radio waves)
- Infrared waves
- Light waves

- Ultraviolet waves
- X-rays
- Gamma rays

Radio waves are usually referred to as RF, standing for *radio frequency*. In the early days of radio, the term *ether* was invented to describe the undetectable medium that carries electromagnetic waves. However, experiments have shown that the ether does not actually exist and no medium is required to carry the waves, which are a form of energy, but you still sometimes hear people refer to radio as "traveling through the ether."

Frequency, Wavelength, and Amplitude

Radio waves come in a range of frequencies and wavelengths. Those used for broadcasting in the United States range from about 500 kHz to 12 GHz. As mentioned for sound, a hertz (Hz) is one cycle of the wave per second. The units used for RF frequencies are as follows:

> kHz   kilo (thousand) hertz
> MHz   mega (million) hertz
> GHz   giga (billion) hertz

Whatever their frequency, all electromagnetic waves travel through a vacuum at the speed of light (about 186,000 miles per second, or 300 million meters per second). This speed is almost the same in air, but it decreases in other materials. Figure 4.1 represents a radio wave as it travels through space; the *wavelength* is the distance that one "wave" or *cycle* of a signal occupies. Waves with short wavelengths have high frequencies, and those with longer wavelengths have lower frequencies. It is easy to calculate the wavelength of a signal if you know its frequency, because the frequency multiplied by the wavelength always equals the speed of light. Therefore, the wavelength in meters is approximately 300 million divided by the frequency.

As shown in the figure, radio waves have an amplitude as well as a frequency—just like sound waves.

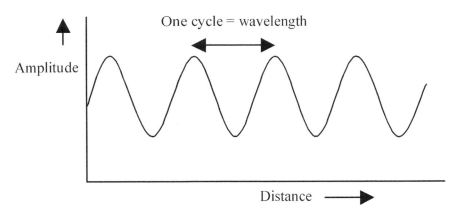

Figure 4.1. Radio Wave

Frequencies, Bands, and Channels

Radio frequency transmissions are divided up into *bands* for different purposes. Let's calculate the wavelength of some typical signals in the main broadcast bands:

MF – Medium Frequency – AM Radio Band (535–1705 kHz)
AM Radio – 1120 kHz
300 million meters/sec ÷ 1120 thousand cycles/sec
= 268 meters, or about 880 feet

VHF – Very High Frequency – FM Radio Band (88–108 MHz)
FM Radio – 98.1 MHz
300 million meters/sec ÷ 98.1 million cycles/sec
= 3 meters, or about 10 feet

VHF – Very High Frequency – Television Band (54–216 MHz)
VHF TV, Channel 8 – 181.25 MHz
300 million meters/sec ÷ 181.25 million cycles/sec
= 1.65 meters, or about 5 feet

UHF – Ultra High Frequency – Television Band (470–806 MHz)
UHF TV, Channel 40 – 627.25 MHz
300 million meters/sec ÷ 627.25 million cycles/sec
= 0.47 meters, or about 18 inches

SHF – Super High Frequency – Broadcasting Satellite Ku Band
(11–14 GHz)

Direct Broadcast Satellite, Transponder 30 – 12.647 GHz
300 million meters/sec ÷ 12.647 billion cycles/sec
  = 2.37 centimeters, or about 1 inch

As this exercise illustrates, the wavelength of an AM radio signal is much longer than the wavelength of an FM radio signal, which is significantly longer than the wavelength of a UHF TV signal. Because of these differing wavelengths, there are big differences between the antenna types used to transmit and receive AM, FM, and TV signals. The wavelengths used for direct broadcast satellites are even shorter, which explains why the antennas used (small dishes) are so different from other types of broadcast antennas.

Each radio band is further divided into *channels*, each with a range of frequencies. The range of frequencies from lowest to highest is known as the channel *bandwidth*. The term may also refer to any particular range of frequencies, not only in RF.

The UHF and SHF bands have further subdivisions, with bands that are used for terrestrial radio links, satellite links, and for satellite broadcasting. These include the L, S, C, X, Ku, K, and Ka bands, with frequencies from about 1 GHz to 40 GHz.

Propagation Properties

Because of the varying wavelengths, waves in different bands have different propagation properties. In particular, the shorter the wavelength, the more the wave tends to travel in straight lines and to be blocked by obstacles in its path. Longer waves, such as in the AM medium frequency band, tend to "flow" around obstructions and propagate in different ways, with a *ground wave* and a *sky wave*. See Chapter 17 for details.

RF Over Wires and Cables

As described previously, RF waves travel through space as electromagnetic waves. However, it is important to understand that the same RF frequencies can be carried as varying electrical voltages over copper wires and cables, just like baseband audio and video signals. However, the distance they can travel over wires is restricted by the signal loss in the cable at RF frequencies.

Modulation

Carriers and Subcarriers

Sound and light waves are baseband signals that carry information that people can hear and see directly, but radio waves are used to carry sound, pictures, and other information over long distances. Therefore, radio waves are often referred to as the *carrier* or *carrier wave*. They carry information by varying one or more of their characteristics: this is called *modulation*. In traditional analog broadcasting, the characteristics that are varied are the amplitude and frequency, but there are several other, more complex, modulation methods used for different purposes, as discussed in the following sections.

The term *subcarrier* has two meanings. It may refer to a modulated carrier that is combined with other signals and then modulated onto a higher carrier frequency. It also sometimes refers to the use of multiple carriers of similar frequencies in one system (e.g., COFDM, as mentioned later in this chapter).

Modulation for the broadcast signal takes place as part of the transmission process (see Chapter 16). A radio or television receiver picks up the transmitted radio waves and selects the correct RF channel with a *tuner*. It then performs *demodulation* in order to recover the program information that was carried by the radio wave, converting it back to baseband audio, video, and perhaps data, signals.

Amplitude Modulation

In *amplitude modulation* transmissions, known as AM, the program information signal is used to modulate (vary) the amplitude of the carrier wave, as illustrated in Figure 4.2. When the amplitude of the program signal is zero, the carrier remains unmodulated. As the instantaneous amplitude of the signal increases up to its maximum, then the carrier amplitude varies accordingly, up to the maximum amount—100 percent modulation.

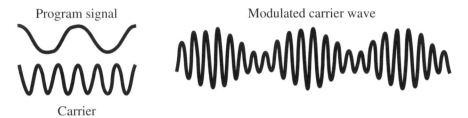

Figure **4.2.** Amplitude Modulation

Frequency Modulation

In *frequency modulation* transmissions, known as FM, the program information signal is used to modulate the frequency of the carrier wave, as illustrated in Figure 4.3. When the amplitude of the program signal is zero, the carrier remains at its original frequency. As the instantaneous amplitude of the signal increases up to its maximum, then the carrier frequency varies accordingly, up to the maximum amount allowed, which is usually 100 percent modulation.

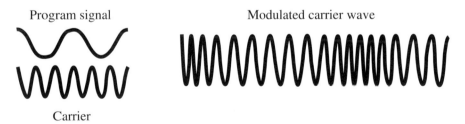

Figure **4.3.** Frequency Modulation

Quadrature Amplitude Modulation

A variant of AM is called *quadrature amplitude modulation*, which is known as QAM. This provides a way to carry additional information in some types of radio and television transmission without using significant extra bandwidth. In particular, it is used to carry supplementary services in AM radio and, with a subcarrier, to carry the chrominance information in NTSC television.

With QAM, two separate signals are modulated onto two separate carriers that are of the same frequency, but one-quarter wavelength out of *phase* with one another, as shown in Figure 4.4. Phase in this regard means the exact timing of arrival of the wave, and one-quarter of a wavelength, is 90 degrees.

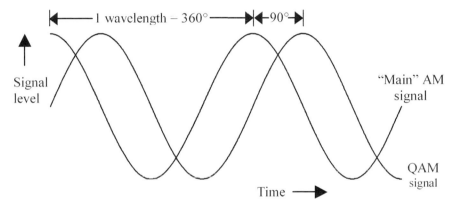

Figure 4.4. Example of Two Waves in Quadrature

The figure shows that when one carrier is at a positive or negative maximum level, the other one is always at zero (half-way between maximum and minimum), and there is always a fixed 90-degree phase offset between the two signals. This fact allows the two carriers to both be modulated with different information, and yet be separately demodulated at the receiver. Having the same frequency, they occupy the same portion of the radio spectrum.

Digital Modulation Systems

Digital broadcasting generally uses more sophisticated modulation systems, including variants of amplitude and frequency modulation, and ones that vary the phase of the wave.

In ATSC digital television, 8-VSB is used—an eight-level amplitude modulation system. This method is discussed further in Chapter 15. Several versions of QAM are used for digital transmission systems (e.g., in AM IBOC radio and digital cable television). In this case, the two carriers are modulated to various discrete levels that, taken together, represent a particular digital *symbol*. There may be different numbers of symbols (typically 16, 64, or 256), depending on the application.

Modulation systems where the phase of the wave is varied, for example the various versions of *phase shift keying (PSK)*, are also used, particularly for digital satellite broadcasting. The theory gets very technical, so we won't cover it here.

Pulse code modulation (PCM) refers to a particular method of carrying signals in digital form. It actually occurs at baseband (e.g., as used for compact discs) although PCM signals may also be modulated onto an RF carrier.

COFDM

Various systems for digital transmission use modulation of multiple carriers to make the signal more robust, particularly so it can resist *multipath* reception conditions. COFDM, the *coded orthogonal frequency division multiplex* system is used for IBOC, DAB, DRM, DVB-T, and ISDB-T broadcasting (as well as for the repeaters used with satellite radio systems), and for electronic newsgathering (ENG) digital radio links.

The COFDM signal is composed of thousands of separate subcarrier frequencies, each of which carries a relatively low-speed digital data stream. Techniques such as *interleaving* and *forward error correction* (FEC) enable a receiver that fails to pick up some of these subcarriers, nevertheless to recover the main signal. This makes the signal very robust and easier to receive under difficult conditions. Again, the theory gets rather technical, so we won't go into further details.

Sidebands

When an RF carrier (or subcarrier) wave of a particular frequency is modulated with a signal of another frequency, the resulting RF signal has additional RF components called *sidebands*. Sideband frequencies are typically the carrier frequency, plus or minus a whole multiple (1×, 2×, etc.) of the modulating frequency. It is these sidebands produced by modulation that carry the actual information in the radio wave.

As an example for AM, a carrier wave of, say, 650 kHz, amplitude modulated with an audio signal of 10 kHz, will produce a composite signal comprising the original carrier of 650 kHz plus an upper sideband of 660 kHz and a lower sideband of 640 kHz. The number and size of the sidebands depends on the type of modulation, but they always extend both above and below the original carrier frequency. In some cases, it is possible to transmit only part of the sidebands and still recover the program information at the receiver. In other cases, the main carrier is suppressed and only the sidebands are transmitted.

This concept of sidebands is important because it affects the amount of radio spectrum, or bandwidth, used for a given type of transmission—this is discussed later in the chapters on broadcast standards.

Light Modulation

For completeness, it should be mentioned that light waves can also be modulated in intensity to carry information. The two most common applications are for film optical sound tracks and for carrying audio, video, and data over fiber-optic links.

CHAPTER 5

Analog Color Television

NTSC

NTSC refers to the National Television System Committee—the committee that designed the standard for today's analog television system, originally adopted in 1941 (monochrome) and 1953 (color). This section explains the principles of television analog video (picture) signals at *baseband* (not modulated onto a carrier). The system for transmitting the signals is explained in Chapter 14.

Frames

NTSC video signals produce a rapid-fire series of still pictures that are shown on a television receiver or monitor. Each of these pictures is called a *frame*. Because of the phenomenon known as persistence of vision, the eye does not see a series of still pictures, but rather an illusion that the picture on the TV is moving.

Figure 5.1 provides a simple example of a series of still pictures that might be used to create the illusion that a ball is bouncing across the screen.

Figure 5.1. Series of Still Pictures That Create Illusion of Motion

The number of complete pictures presented to the viewer every second is known as the *refresh rate*. If the refresh rate is too low, then any motion on the screen appears to be jerky because the frames do not appear fast enough to maintain persistence of vision;

this is known as *judder*. When cinematography was developed, it was found that a rate of 24 frames per second was enough for reasonably smooth motion portrayal, and that rate has been used for film all over the world ever since. Later, when television was developed, in the United Kingdom a rate of 25 frames per second was selected and 30 frames per second was selected in the United States.

Scanning

In the NTSC system, each video picture frame is "painted" on the television screen, from top to bottom, one horizontal line at a time. This process is called *scanning*. In NTSC, there are 525 horizontal lines in each frame, 483 of which form the actual picture. The refresh rate is 30 frames per second.

Interlacing

When the NTSC standard was developed, 30 frames of video per second was about the best that available technology could process and transmit in a 6 MHz-wide television *transmission channel*. However, pictures presented at 30 frames per second appear to flicker terribly. NTSC television reduces this flicker without actually increasing the frame rate by using an arrangement called *interlacing*. There are 525 horizontal lines in each frame, but, with interlacing, they are not presented in successive order (i.e., 1, 2, 3, . . . , etc.). Instead, all of the odd-numbered lines are presented first, followed by all of the even-numbered lines. The odd and even line images that are created during the interlacing process are called *fields*. Two fields make up a frame, and they interlace together to form the complete picture, as illustrated in Figure 5.2. Because the picture rate is 30 frames per second, the field rate is 60 fields per second.

In an interlaced NTSC picture, each of the lines in the picture is still refreshed 30 times every second. However, the human eye cannot perceive the fact that two adjacent lines on the video screen are

Field A-1   Field A-2

Frame A

Figure 5.2. Two Interlaced Fields for Each NTSC Frame

being refreshed at different times when there is only a period of
1/60th of a second between them. The effect is to create the appearance that the full screen is being refreshed twice as often, or 60
times per second, increasing the apparent refresh rate and greatly
reducing the perceived screen flicker.

Film Projection

Just as a comparison, we will explain how flicker is reduced for
cinema film that is projected onto a screen at 24 frames per second.
Film projectors use a rotating *shutter* to interrupt the light beam
while each film frame is moved into position for projection. The
shutter is normally fitted with two blades rather than one, thus

interrupting the light twice for each projected frame. This produces an apparent refresh rate of 48 times per second, which greatly reduces the perceived screen flicker.

Progressive Scan

If interlacing is not used with a television picture, then each frame is painted on the screen, from top to bottom, in its entirety. This is called *progressive scan* and is not used for NTSC. Progressive scan is used with video for computer monitors and for some digital television formats. In that case, much higher frame rates are needed if flicker is to be avoided. This also improves motion portrayal. Fortunately, with computer systems it is actually less complex to implement higher frame rate noninterlaced pictures than it is to implement interlacing.

Active Video and Blanking

As previously mentioned, there are 525 horizontal lines of information in an NTSC video signal, 483 of which are the *active video* lines that carry the actual picture information. The other lines make up the *vertical blanking interval*. Even the active video lines do not carry picture information for their entire duration, but have a period at the beginning and end of the line known as the *horizontal blanking interval*. The reason for these blanking intervals relates to the way *cathode ray tube* (CRT) television displays, and older-technology television cameras with tube-type light sensors, work.

With CRT displays, an *electron gun* inside the CRT is the device that actually paints the video picture. It shoots a beam of *electrons* (the smallest unit of electricity) inside the tube onto the back of the screen. This causes little dots of chemicals on the screen, called *phosphors*, to generate light. Variations in the strength of the electron beam cause the phosphor to produce different levels of brightness, corresponding to the content of the original scene.

As shown in Figure 5.3, the beam of electrons from the electron gun moves in a left-to-right, top-to-bottom manner. Each time the beam reaches the right edge of the picture screen, it must stop and then move back to the left-hand side of the screen in order to start painting the next line. If the electron gun were to remain on during this entire process, it would paint a line of the picture on the screen and then immediately paint a streak right below it while it *retraced* its path back to the left side of the screen. In order to prevent this from happening, the electron gun is turned off after it reaches the far right side of the screen, and it remains off until the beam is positioned back on the left side of the screen and is ready to begin painting the next line. The period when the electron gun is off, while it is retracing its route over the screen, is the horizontal blanking interval. It is a very short period of time, significantly less than it takes to actually paint one horizontal line of video on the screen.

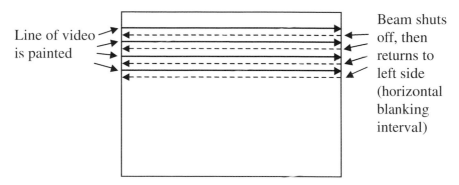

Figure 5.3. Horizontal Line Scan and Blanking

The same concern about putting a streak on the screen must be addressed when the electron beam finishes painting the bottom line of video and needs to be repositioned to the top left-hand corner of the screen to start a new field. During this operation, the beam is once again turned off while it is retargeted toward the upper left corner, as shown in Figure 5.4. This period when the beam is turned off is the vertical blanking interval or VBI.

The VBI lasts as long as it takes to paint 21 lines on the screen. These VBI line periods are referred to by their line numbers but contain no picture information. There are 21 VBI lines transmitted before the beginning of each field of video information, 42 in total—hence the 483 active video lines in a 525-line NTSC signal. Because there is no picture information on the VBI lines, some of them can be used to carry additional, nonvideo information, as listed on page 227 in Chapter 14.

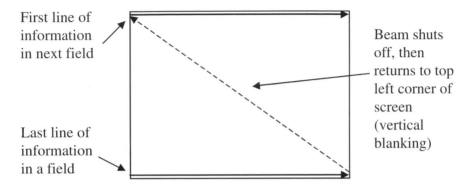

First line of information in next field

Beam shuts off, then returns to top left corner of screen (vertical blanking)

Last line of information in a field

Figure 5.4. Vertical Blanking

The previous explanation of blanking relates to tube-type picture displays, which have been used since the early days of television. However, the types of television cameras that use tubes as the light-sensing (*pickup*) device also rely on the blanking periods to allow the electron beam, which scans the light-sensitive target in the tube, to retrace to the beginning of each line and field. Most modern cameras use pickup devices such as *charge-coupled devices* (CCDs), and modern picture displays often use *liquid crystal display* (LCD) and *plasma* screens; these do not, in fact, require blanking intervals for beam retrace. However, to maintain compatibility with all existing devices, the NTSC video blanking timing remains unchanged, and, in any case, some of the NTSC VBI lines are also used for other purposes, as mentioned above. Note that digital television does not include the VBI in the transmitted signal because the picture encoding system is completely different from NTSC (see Chapter 15).

Synchronizing Pulses

So that equipment using the video signals can be synchronized, both within itself and with other equipment, it is necessary to indicate the start of each frame of video and when each line begins. This is done with *synchronizing pulses*, usually known as *sync pulses*. A *horizontal sync pulse* marks the beginning of every line, and a series of broad and narrow pulses extending over several lines marks the start of each new field.

Video Waveform

Let's now look at the actual video signal that carries the picture information, starting with the camera at the beginning of the chain. Typically, a television camera is focused on a scene, and the image is then dissected into scan lines and repetitively into fields and frames. As shown in Figure 5.5, the camera produces a video signal with a varying voltage on its output. The voltage is proportional to the amount of light at each point in the picture, with the lowest voltage being equivalent to black and the highest voltage being equivalent to the brightest parts of the picture. At the beginning of each line and field, the camera adds horizontal and vertical sync pulses, so that all equipment using that signal will know where the

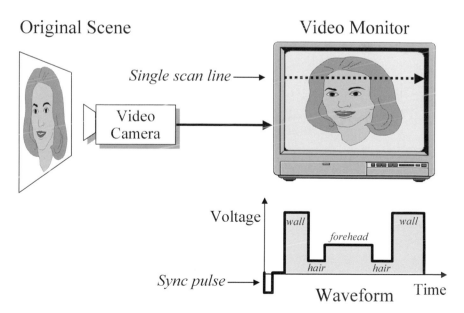

Figure 5.5. Monochrome Scan Line Waveform

lines and fields begin. When this video signal of picture information and sync pulses is fed to a picture monitor, it produces pictures. When it is displayed on a special piece of test equipment (*waveform monitor*) to show the shape of the electrical signal, it is known as a *video waveform*.

Luminance, Chrominance, and Composite Video

The simple explanation above works well if the camera is only producing a black-and-white image based on the brightness, or *luminance*, of the scene. However, color cameras actually generate three separate signals for the three primary colors of red, green, and blue. It would be wasteful and difficult to route and transmit these three separate R, G, and B signals; therefore, the NTSC standard defines how they should be combined together. This is done by adding R, G, and B in the correct proportions to make the luminance signal, which is always referred to as Y. Then, by subtracting the luminance from each of the red and blue signals, two *color difference* signals are produced, called R-Y and B-Y. These two signals are called *chrominance*. Because the eye is less sensitive to color detail than to brightness, the chrominance signals have their *bandwidth* reduced to make it possible to transmit color in the same transmission channel as black-and-white television. They are then *modulated* using QAM (see Chapter 4) onto a *chrominance subcarrier*, also known as a *color subcarrier*. The subcarrier chrominance signal is added to the luminance signal, as they both can be carried on the same cable from the camera and around the studio, and ultimately transmitted over-the-air. The resulting signal that combines luminance and chrominance picture information with sync pulses, all carried together on one cable, is known as *composite video*.

Strictly speaking, the electrical video signal components carried through most of the television chain should be referred to as *luma* and *chroma*. These terms have a slightly different technical meaning compared to luminance and chrominance (it has to do with something called *gamma correction*, which is outside the scope of this book). However, the terms are frequently used interchangeably— although sometimes incorrectly—by most people. Therefore, for simplicity, we will only use luminance and chrominance in this book, except where normal usage is to use the words luma or chroma.

Figure 5.6 shows an example of a composite color waveform carrying the well-known test signal *color bars*. The illustration shows how this signal looks on a waveform monitor; on a picture monitor, all that is seen is vertical bands of color. You can see that each bar has a different level of luminance (brightness), and the chrominance signal, superimposed onto each bar, carries the color information for that bar. The horizontal sync pulse is at the beginning of each line. The short burst of subcarrier that can be seen after the sync pulse is in the horizontal blanking period, so it is not visible; it is needed to help the receiver decode the chrominance information.

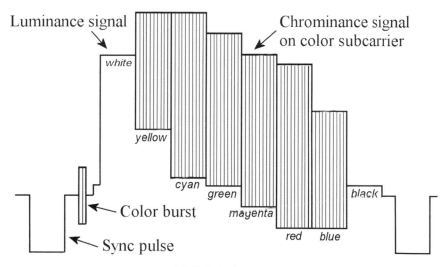

Figure 5.6. NTSC Color Bars Waveform

Decoding at the Receiver

At the television receiver, after passing through the transmission chain, the composite NTSC signal is decoded. The receiver separates the luminance and color difference signals and, by adding and subtracting these values, the receiver can again produce red, green, and blue signals. These drive the display device (e.g., the electron gun of a CRT) to produce the red, green, and blue parts of the picture, which are built up line by line and frame by frame, that the viewer's eye sees as the original scene.

Actual NTSC Frame and Field Rates

The 30 frames per second and 60 fields per second values were defined when the NTSC standard was written for black-and-white television. When the color subcarrier was introduced to carry the chrominance information for color television, it was found necessary to change the frame and field rates slightly (by a factor of just one part per thousand) to help avoid interference with the black-and-white picture and the transmitted audio signal. The actual values used today for NTSC are therefore 29.97 frames per second and 59.94 fields per second.

PAL and SECAM

The PAL and SECAM color systems used in many other countries work similarly to NTSC, with the main differences described as follows.

Scanning Formats

NTSC has 525 total lines per picture and 30 frames per second, whereas in most countries PAL and SECAM have 625 total lines and 25 frames per second (525/30 for PAL in Brazil).

PAL

The PAL color subcarrier chroma signal has a different frequency from NTSC and reverses *phase* on alternate lines. In the early days of color television, this resulted in less chroma error and more accurate color pictures. With much more stable modern NTSC equipment, this advantage has largely disappeared. There are also minor differences in the way the color difference signals are derived and processed.

SECAM

In SECAM, the color difference signals, instead of being transmitted together, are transmitted on sequential lines, and a memory is used to make them available at the time required. In addition, the color subcarrier is modulated with FM rather than QAM.

Because of difficulties with processing SECAM signals, countries that use SECAM for transmission almost always produce their programs in the PAL standard and convert to SECAM just before transmission.

Channel Bandwidth

NTSC is transmitted in a 6 MHz-wide television channel, whereas PAL and SECAM are usually transmitted in a 7 MHz or 8 MHz channel, depending on the country.

HD Analog Video

High definition video, usually known as HD, is generally associated with digital television. However, all cameras and picture displays, including those for HD, operate as analog devices when the images are first acquired and finally displayed. This is because the light from the original scene, and the light produced by the final display device, is itself analog, so the associated video voltage at that point is also analog.

Analog high definition video formats are usually referred to with the same terms used for the digital HD formats (1080I and 720P). They are often used to feed picture monitors and video projectors, and may be carried as follows:

- *RGB* signals: one cable each for red, green, and blue signals
- *YPbPr* component signals: one cable for the luminance, Y, and one cable for each of the color difference signals known as Pb and Pr

With RGB, the sync pulses may be carried on the green channel or may be carried on one or two additional cables: for horizontal and vertical sync. With YPbPr components, the sync pulses are always carried on the Y channel. HD signals use *trilevel sync*, with three levels, rather than the usual two, showing where the different parts of the signal start and finish.

The RGB or YPbPr signals are referred to as *component video* because the three colors, or the luminance and color difference signals, are kept separate. This is an important concept, both for analog and digital video. High definition video is always component; there is no such thing as high definition composite video.

CHAPTER 6

Digital Audio and Video

This chapter discusses the basics of *baseband* digital audio and video as typically used in studio facilities. Using digital, rather than analog, signals in the studio results in higher audio and video quality, greater production capabilities, and more efficient operations—whether they ultimately feed either analog or digital transmission systems.

It should be noted that the terms *digital radio* and *digital television* are usually used to mean the method of transmission of the audio and video signals. It is, in fact, possible for such digital transmitters to be fed with signals produced in a basically analog studio facility and converted to digital for transmission. For maximum quality, however, it is desirable that both transmission and studios should be digital.

Digital Audio

When we speak of *digital audio*, we are referring to audio signals that have been converted into a series of *binary numbers* (using just the digits 0 and 1, see Chapter 7) rather than being sent as a continuously variable *analog waveform*. The advantage of this scheme is that binary numbers can be easily processed by computers and other digital equipment, and can be distributed and recorded with great accuracy. Therefore, digital audio is typically not subject to any of the degradations of analog audio (e.g., noise and distortion)—even after being copied many times, and going through a long chain of equipment.

There are five basic concepts that one needs to grasp in order to have an understanding of digital audio: *sampling*, *quantizing*, *resolution*, *bitstream*, and *bit rate*.

Sampling

Figure 6.1 shows an analog waveform plot of the amplitude of an audio signal as it varies in time. In an *analog-to-digital* converter, the amplitude of the wave is measured at regular intervals: this is called sampling. Each individual sample represents the level of the audio signal at a particular instant in time.

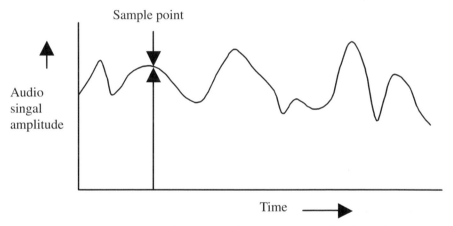

Figure 6.1. Digital Sample of an Analog Audio Signal

The *sampling rate* is the rate at which digital samples are made from the original material. The more often the original material is sampled, the more accurately the digital signal represents the original material.

Figure 6.2 shows an analog signal being sampled at some regular interval. Figure 6.3 shows the same analog signal being sampled twice as often. As can be seen by comparing these two figures, the more often a signal is digitally sampled, the closer the representation will be.

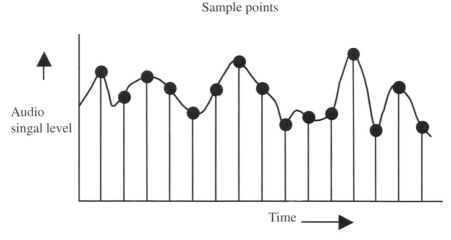

Figure 6.2. Periodic Digital Samples of an Analog Signal

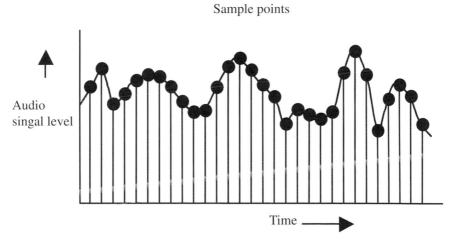

Figure 6.3. More Frequent Digital Samples of an Analog Signal

Four main sampling rates are used for digital audio: 32,000 samples per second, 44,100 samples per second, 48,000 samples per second, and 96,000 samples per second. Usually they are referred to simply as 32 kHz, 44.1 kHz, 48 kHz, and 96 kHz, respectively. Audio compact discs (CDs) have a digital sampling rate of 44.1 kHz, but most broadcast digital audio studio equipment uses 48 kHz sampling.

Quantizing

The audio samples are converted to a series of binary numbers, ranging from 0 to the largest binary number used for the system. For each sample, the number nearest in size to the analog amplitude is used. This is known as quantizing.

Resolution

The resolution of digital audio is the precision with which the sampled audio is measured. In other words, how accurately the digital audio numbers match the original analog material. Like many aspects of digital systems, resolution is measured in *bits*, because they comprise binary numbers. The higher the number of bits, the more accurately the digital signal represents the original analog material. CDs and many other items of equipment use 16 bits to represent each audio sample.

Sixteen-bit audio is not twice as accurate as 8 bit audio in replicating the original analog material: it is 256 times better. In Chapter 7, we will learn that adding one more bit to each sample number doubles the accuracy of that number; therefore, a 9 bit sample would be twice as accurate as 8 bits, and 10 bits would be twice as accurate as 9 bits. Continuing in this way, it can be seen that 16 bits is 256 times more accurate than 8 bits.

Bitstream and Bit Rate

When binary numbers representing the audio samples are sent down a wire one after the other, the stream of binary digits (bits) is referred to as a *serial bitstream* or usually just as a bitstream.

The bit rate necessary to transport a digital audio signal is directly related to the digital resolution of the digital audio and its sampling rate. Using the digital resolution and the sampling rate for CDs, for example, we can calculate the bit rate necessary to transport CD audio:

CD digital resolution: 16 bits/sample
× CD sampling rate: 44,100 samples/second

= CD bit rate per channel:	705,600 bits/second/channel
× 2 stereo channels:	2
= total CD bit rate:	1,411,200 bits per second or about 1.4 Mbps

There are eight bits in each *byte* of data. So, in order to store one second of CD stereo audio on a computer disk, we need 1,411,200 ÷ 8 = 176,400 bytes of disk space. A typical three-minute song, uncompressed, would require 176,400 bytes × 180 seconds = 31.752 Megabytes of disk space. Compression techniques for reducing the bit rate and size of audio files are covered later in the book. For more on bits and bytes, see Chapter 7.

Audio A/D and D/A Converters

The process described previously is carried out in an *analog-to-digital* (A/D) converter. The process can be reversed in a *digital-to-analog* (D/A) converter, which then re-creates an analog audio waveform from the digital bitstream. These converters may be stand-alone units or may be inside other equipment.

It is common for equipment that uses digital signals internally, such as a *digital audio tape* (DAT) recorder, to have A/D and D/A converters inside the unit. This means that the external interfaces, or connections to the outside world, can be either digital or analog. This gives much greater flexibility in making system interconnections, which can be either analog or digital. As an example, a consumer CD player, which plays back digital audio from the disc, usually connects to a stereo system through analog left and right channel connections. However, the same player may have a digital *coaxial* or *optical* audio output, which can feed a home theater system with higher-quality digital signals. Similarly, professional digital audio equipment can usually work in either all-digital systems or as part of a mixed analog/digital environment.

Every A/D and D/A conversion introduces a small quality loss. Therefore, for highest quality, the number of conversions backward and forward between analog and digital audio should be kept to a minimum.

AES/EBU Digital Audio Distribution Standard

The *AES/EBU* digital audio format, also known as AES3, is a standardized format for transporting uncompressed digital audio from place to place, and is the most common standard used for this purpose. AES/EBU refers to the Audio Engineering Society and the European Broadcasting Union organizations, respectively, which together developed and published the standard.

In order to transport digital audio information, a stream of digital bits must be carried from the originating point to the receiving point. So that the device receiving the bits can understand which ones belong where, a standardized format for transporting the bits must be defined. This is what AES/EBU does. The format is able to carry two channels of audio (either two mono channels or one stereo pair), at any of the standard digital audio sampling frequencies, and with an accuracy of 16, 20, or 24 bits per sample.

The stream of digital bits is organized into 64 bit segments called *frames* (not to be confused with video picture frames). Each of these frames is further broken down into two subframes. Subframe 1 carries the digital audio information for audio channel 1, and subframe 2 carries the digital audio information for audio channel 2. In the vast majority of radio stations broadcasting music, the two subframes correspond to the left and right channels of the stereo audio pair. The AES/EBU frame structure is illustrated in Figure 6.4. The audio data is sent using a system called *pulse code modulation* (PCM), and this type of uncompressed audio is often known as *linear PCM*.

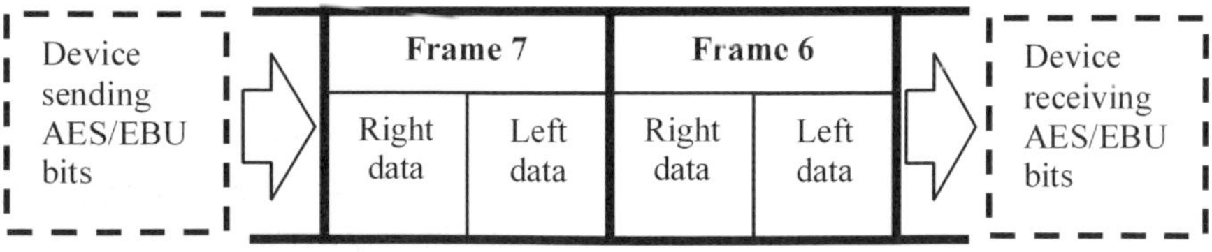

Figure 6.4. AES/EBU Digital Audio Frame Structure

AES/EBU signals can be carried over *twisted pair* or *coaxial* cables, or on *fiber-optic* cables. They may also be combined (embedded) with video signals, and may also be sent on some types of RF-based distribution systems. It is important to understand that the AES/EBU standard only defines the way digital audio is transported from one point to another, it does not define the format for audio storage, which is covered in Chapter 8.

SPDIF

Another digital interface you may come across is the Sony/Philips Digital Interface (SPDIF). This may use either coaxial or fiber-optic cables. It can carry a linear PCM AES/EBU signal, but it is also specified to carry a compressed audio bitstream such as *Dolby AC-3*, which may include *5.1 channel surround sound* (see page 245 in Chapter 15).

Digital Signal Robustness

Digital signals are much more robust than analog and retain their quality though multiple recordings and transmission. The reason for this is that digital equipment only has to store and reproduce 0s (low level) and 1s (high level) for the data. It does not need to accurately reproduce all of the levels between low and high as it would for analog. To see how this works, let's look at a recording on a digital tape machine (this applies to both audio and video, so it could be either).

Figure 6.5 shows a string of 0s and 1s as they might be recorded on tape, represented by high and low signal levels. So long as the tape player can distinguish between the high and low levels, the signal read off the tape will be precisely the same as the series of 0s and 1s that was recorded. Drawing (a) shows the digital signal with a small amount of noise, represented by the variable dark line (the *tape hiss* that would be heard on an analog audio tape machine). Drawing (b) shows the same signal with a much larger amount of noise—half the amplitude of the wanted signal. In an analog system, this amount of noise would be unbearable, almost drowning out the wanted signal but, as is clear from the drawing,

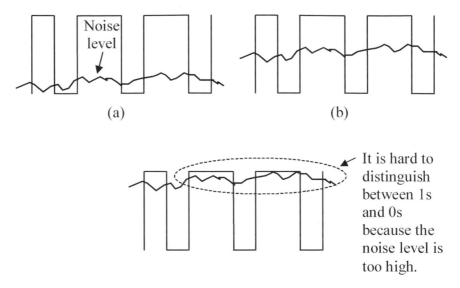

Figure 6.5. How a Digital Signal Relates to Noise

it is still easy to detect the 0s and 1s and recover them perfectly. Only when the level increases greatly, as shown in the lower drawing, does it become impossible to accurately detect the digital signal, because it becomes too hard to be sure when the level is intended to be a 0 or a 1. Such digital signals, whether audio or video, are therefore much less affected by any noise introduced in a recording device or transmission path.

SD and HD Digital Video

Each line in an analog NTSC video picture is a continuous stream of video information. In contrast, each line in a digital video picture can be considered as a series of discrete *pixels*, derived from the words *picture element*. The basic principles of converting baseband analog video to digital video are in many ways similar to the digital audio conversion described previously. The analog video waveform of every line in every frame is sampled at a suitable rate and resolution, as illustrated in Figure 6.6. As with digital audio, the video samples are converted into a series of binary numbers; they are then coded in a special way, and finally produce a serial digital video bitstream.

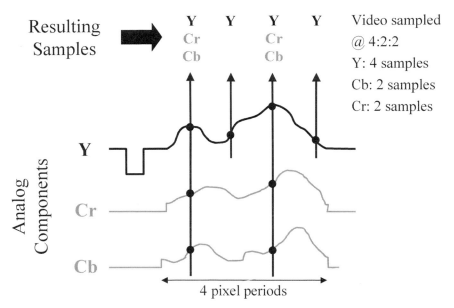

Figure 6.6. Digital Video Sampling at 4:2:2

Digital Components and Color Subsampling

Modern digital video systems sample the *luminance* and *color difference* video component signals separately, and produce *digital component* video signals. This allows much higher picture quality to be maintained compared to NTSC *composite video*. Once in the digital domain, special methods can be used to send the separate components in order, one after the other, down a single wire, thus maintaining the single-wire convenience of composite video.

As with NTSC video, the color difference signals can have their bandwidth reduced, to save on transmission and storage bandwidth. This is done by sampling the color difference signals less often than the luminance signals, and is known as *chroma subsampling*. A typical arrangement, which is shown in Figure 6.6, is 4:2:2 sampling. This means that for every four luminance samples, there are two samples for each of the color difference signals. Other arrangements include 4:1:1 and 4:2:0, where the chroma samples are reduced further in the horizontal or vertical directions; and 4:4:4, where the red, green, and blue signals are all sampled equally.

Digital Video Formats

Analog video signals produced by 525-line cameras, as used for NTSC television, can be sampled and converted into digital video. This process produces one of the *standard definition* DTV formats. However, because the DTV transmission standard includes a method for *compressing* the transmitted video, it allows more video information to be squeezed into the same transmission channel size as used for analog television. This provides several opportunities for new and improved video formats that were not available with the NTSC standard. Specifically, it allows for higher *resolution* pictures, with wider *aspect ratio* and, in some cases, with higher *frame rates* and/or *progressive scan*.

The ATSC digital television standard defines 18 different picture formats for transmission (36 if the same formats using the small frame rate adjustment mentioned later are counted). Only a small number of them are usually used by broadcasters. Like NTSC video signals, all of the digital video formats end up as a rapid-fire series of still pictures that are displayed by a television receiver, but there are significant differences from NTSC video. The main characteristics of a digital video format are as follows:

• Number of active lines per picture
• Number of active pixels per line
• Frame rate
• Interlaced or progressive scan
• Picture aspect ratio

The video production formats (i.e., those used by cameras and recorders, etc.) most likely to be found in broadcast facilities are the following:

High Definition
1080 lines × 1920 pixels, 30 frames per second, interlaced, 16:9 aspect ratio
(usually referred to as 1080I)
1080 lines × 1920 pixels, 24 frames per second, progressive, 16:9 aspect ratio
(usually referred to as 1080P/24)

720 lines × 1280 pixels, 60 frames per second, progressive, 16:9
   aspect ratio
(usually referred to as 720P)
720 lines × 1280 pixels, 24 frames per second, progressive, 16:9
   aspect ratio
(usually referred to as 720P/24)

Standard Definition
483 lines × 720 pixels, 60 frames per second, progressive, 16:9
   aspect ratio
483 lines × 720 pixels, 30 frames per second, interlaced, 16:9 aspect
   ratio
483 lines × 720 pixels, 30 frames per second, interlaced, 4:3 aspect
   ratio

The high definition (HD) formats have 1080 or 720 lines, and the
standard definition (SD) formats all have 483 lines. The numbers
of lines and pixels for the SD production formats are slightly different from those actually transmitted in ATSC DTV, but this is not
significant for most purposes. The last format listed is the direct
digital equivalent of analog NTSC video and is often referred to as
601 video—from the ITU (International Telecommunications Union)
BT. 601 standard for 525- and 625-line digital video sampling and
format.

For various reasons—mainly to do with transferring programs into
different formats for distribution in different markets—there is an
increasing move to produce some types of programs at 24 frames
per second, the same as film rate. This frame rate is therefore
common in many high definition production and postproduction
facilities.

Let's look further at these various digital video characteristics.

Lines and Pixels

These numbers largely determine the *resolution* of the picture (i.e.,
how much detail it can display and how sharp the picture looks).

For digital video, the number of lines is the number of active lines in the picture (excluding the vertical blanking interval), and each line is divided up into pixels. A pixel may be considered as a dot on a video screen, the smallest component of a video image. Pixels have become familiar to most computer users because the resolution of a computer screen (i.e., the level of detail on the screen) is usually defined in terms of pixels. Some typical computer screen resolutions, defined in terms of horizontal and vertical pixels, are 640×480 and 1024×768. The more pixels there are on the screen, given a fixed monitor size, the more detailed and sharper looking the image will be. There is a trade-off, though: the larger the numbers of lines and pixels per frame, the more data is needed to transmit or store the video image.

The highest definition ATSC video format has 1080 lines on the screen. Each of these lines contains 1920 pixels, so there are about 2 million pixels in total. The standard definition ATSC video format has 483 lines, each with 720 pixels, so there are about 340,000 pixels in total. This is why it is sometimes said that high definition television is six times as sharp as standard definition. In fact, when compared to NTSC standard definition video, the difference is even greater because the analog NTSC system does not carry the full resolution of digital SD video.

Frame Rate

There are three standard frame rates for ATSC digital video: 24, 30, and 60 frames per second. Twenty-four frames per second is the rate commonly used for film, and this may be used for video carrying film-originated material or, more recently, for actual video production. Thirty frames per second is the same as the rate used for NTSC video. Sixty frames per second is a faster frame rate that improves motion rendition and reduces screen flicker by refreshing the video screen more often. The disadvantage is that the more frames per second that are transmitted, the more data that is needed to transmit or store the video signal.

All of these frame rates are used for transmission. The 30 and 24 frames per second rates with progressive scan may, in some cases, be used for production, but they are not used for display at the receiver because, as previously mentioned, the picture would flicker unacceptably. In these cases, the receiver converts these signals to either 30 frames per second interlaced or, in some cases, to 60 frames per second progressive, for display to the viewer.

At least for the duration of the transition to digital television, most television facilities will be using frame rates that are one part per thousand smaller than the integer frame rates listed previously. They do this to facilitate conversion of NTSC pictures with a frame rate of 29.97 frames per second (see page 42) to digital video for ATSC transmission and to avoid the complication of having multiple timing signals in a single facility.

Interlacing

Each of the three frame rates in ATSC video can be employed with either interlaced or progressive scanning, except that the 1920 × 1080 format is not available with 60 frames per second, progressive, and the 1280 × 720 format is available only with progressive scan.

There has been much debate over whether interlaced or progressive scanning is preferable for digital television. It is generally accepted that 60 frames per second progressive scan video produces the best motion rendition, and this has an advantage for high-motion programming such as sports. However, in the ATSC standard, the maximum resolution format possible with 60 frames per second progressive has 720 lines because, at the time the standard was developed, the bandwidth required for 1080 progressive lines at 60 frames per second was too great to be recorded or transmitted. Under critical viewing conditions, particularly with diagonal lines and/or high motion, some interlacing *artifacts* may be visible with 1080I. In reality, both 1080I (interlaced) and 720P (progressive) formats are capable of producing extremely high-quality pictures, and the choice of whether to use interlaced video or noninterlaced video at a broadcast facility is, to some extent, a question of personal preference.

Aspect Ratio

Two picture aspect ratios, 4:3 and 16:9, as shown in Figure 6.7, are specified in the ATSC standard and are used for digital video.

4:3   16:9

NTSC or ATSC   ATSC

Figure 6.7. 4:3 and 16:9 Aspect Ratios

The 4:3 width to height ratio was selected because it is the same as used in NTSC video, and a tremendous number of archived television programs are in this format. The 16:9 ratio was selected for all high definition programming and, optionally, for standard definition. It was to some extent a compromise between the motion picture industry's desire for as wide a screen as possible and the manufacturing costs of tube-based displays. About 80 percent of motion pictures are shot at an aspect ratio of 1.85:1, which easily fits into a 16:9 screen with negligible use of *letterboxing* (a technique used to fit a video image onto a television screen, without altering the aspect ratio of the original video image, by blacking out the top and bottom portions of the frame).

Bit Rates

Typical figures for sampling and bit rates of digital video in the studio are as follows:

High Definition Video
Sampling rate: 74.25 Mhz

Resolution: 10 bits
Samples per pixel: 2 (average for 4:2:2 sampling)
Total HD bit rate: 74.25 × 10 × 2 = 1.485 Gigabits per second

Standard Definition Video
Sampling rate: 13.5 MHz
Resolution: 10 bits
Samples per pixel: 2 (average for 4:2:2 sampling)
Total SD bit rate: 13.5 × 10 × 2 = 270 Megabits per second

Remember that, in both cases, these are the bit rates for raw, uncompressed digital video. By using *compression* (discussed in Chapter 15), these rates may be greatly reduced for transmission or recording.

Video A/D and D/A Converters

As with audio, the video analog-to-digital conversion processes are carried out in A/D and D/A converters, again working in either direction. As before, these may be stand-alone units or may be inside other items of equipment.

It is common for equipment that uses digital signals internally, such as a *digital videotape recorder* (DVTR), to have A/D and D/A converters combined with other processes inside the unit. This means that the external interfaces, or connections to the outside world, can be either digital or analog. Again, this gives much greater flexibility in making system interconnections, which can be either analog or digital. As an example, a standard definition digital VTR, which records and plays back digital video from the tape, may be incorporated into either an analog or digital video distribution system. However, modern HD video systems usually use digital distribution throughout (remember there is no such thing as a single-wire analog composite HD signal).

Every A/D and D/A conversion introduces a small quality loss. Therefore, for highest quality, the number of conversions backward and forward between analog and digital video should be kept to a minimum.

SMPTE Serial Digital Interfaces

Standards for transporting uncompressed digital video from one place to another in a broadcast studio are set by the Society of Motion Picture and Television Engineers (SMPTE), which has also developed many of the other standards on which television relies. *SMPTE 259M* specifies the serial digital interface (SDI) for SD video, and *SMPTE 292M* specifies the high definition serial digital interface (HD-SDI) for HD video.

The HD-SDI or SDI format carries the stream of digital bits representing the luminance and chrominance samples for the video. The analog sync pulses are not digitized, so special codes are added showing the start of active video (SAV) and end of active video (EAV). The luminance and chrominance data is combined together, and finally the stream of digital bits is sent sequentially down the cable. HD-SDI and SDI are similar in the way they work; the main difference is the much higher bit rate needed for HD-SDI.

Using these standards, digital video signals can be carried over coaxial cables, or over much longer distances using fiber-optic cable. They may also be sent on some types of RF-based distribution systems. It is important to understand that the SDI and HD-SDI standards only define the way digital video is transported from one point to another; they do not define the formats for storage on videotape and servers, which are covered in Chapter 9.

There are other SMPTE and DVB standards for transporting compressed video bitstreams, as mentioned in the section on bitstream distribution in Chapter 9.

CHAPTER 7

Information Technology

Broadcasting today is heavily dependent on computers and the associated information technology. This is partly for regular office programs used for station management, and partly for the specialized software applications that are increasingly used for systems such as program planning, traffic, electronic newsrooms, and station automation. In addition, much of the equipment used for processing digital audio and digital video is based on computer technology. Also, as we learned in the previous chapters, digital audio and digital video signals are defined using the same terms used for computer data. For all of these reasons, it is worth going over some of the basic terms and components that relate to the information technology side of broadcast engineering.

All computer systems and networks, including the Internet, use *bits* to process, store, and carry different types of information, whether it is a text document, numerical spreadsheet, database, graphics, audio recording, or moving pictures. All of these types of information can be coded as a series of numbers, which is how they become types of digital data. So let's start with the numbering system used and what we actually mean by bits and *bytes*.

Binary

Binary Numbers

The regular decimal numbering system that we use every day has ten digits, 0 to 9, and when counting, we carry (add) 1 to the next column each time we reach the largest digit, which is 9. In electronic circuits, it's much easier if we only have to deal with two states—off/on or low/high—rather than ten states, so nearly all digital systems use a numbering system called *binary* that only needs two digits: 0 and 1. When counting in binary, we still add 1 to the next column each time we reach the largest digit, in this case 1. Counting up from 0, the first few binary numbers are as shown in Table 7.1, with the equivalent regular decimal numbers alongside.

Table 7.1. Binary and Decimal Numbers

Binary	Decimal
0	0
1	1
10	2
11	3
100	4
101	5
110	6
111	7
1000	8
1001	9
1011	10

You can see that any decimal number has an equivalent binary number, and it is easy to convert between the two systems. You will also notice that each time we add one more digit column to the binary number, it allows us to double the decimal numbers, or amount of information, that can be coded in binary.

Bits and Bytes

Each binary number consists of a series of 0s and 1s—known as *binary digits*; these words have been combined into the single term *bits* (the abbreviation for "bit" is "b"). Binary numbers are often divided up into groups of eight bits, which are known as *bytes* (the abbreviation for "byte" is "B").

Units for Data Transmission and Storage

When binary data is sent from one place to another, an important consideration is how fast the bits are transmitted. This is measured in bits per second (bps), thousands of (kilo) bits per second (kbps), millions of (mega) bits per second (Mbps), or billions of (giga) bits per second (Gbps).

When data is stored, the usual measure is the capacity in bytes, and it is usually counted in powers of two, because it is based on binary numbers. In this case, the kilobyte unit is slightly larger than one thousand, because it actually refers to 1024 (2^{10}) bytes. The abbreviation is KB (note that the upper-case K is used to indicate 1024, whereas lower-case k always indicates 1000). However, for all the larger storage units, such as megabyte (MB), the same upper-case abbreviation is used whether it is intended to indicate a number based on binary (in this case 1,048,576 or 2^{20}) or decimal (in this case a million).

Data Bandwidth

Somewhat confusingly, the rate at which data can be sent over a particular distribution or transmission medium is often referred to as its *bandwidth*. Note that this is not the same as the analog bandwidth of a channel referred to in Chapter 4. There is no fixed relationship between the analog bandwidth of a channel and the digital data rate it can handle. It depends very much on the method of coding used for carrying the digital data (although there are limits imposed by the fundamental laws of science and mathematics).

Computers

Personal Computers

The personal computer, or PC, is familiar to most people. It is a general-purpose machine that can process very large numbers of bits very quickly to carry out many different tasks, depending on the software that is loaded on it. The main hardware components include all or most of the following:

- Central processing unit (CPU)
- Random access memory (RAM)
- Mass storage: disk drives, etc.
- User interface: keyboard, mouse, picture monitor, loudspeakers
- Graphics subsystem
- Sound subsystem
- Modem for telephone line interface (if needed)
- Network interface (if needed)

The various components may be combined into one compact unit, as in a laptop computer, or may be in several individual components, as in a desktop computer. In broadcast studios, computers may also be built into *rack-mount* units for convenient mounting in equipment racks.

Computer software includes the *operating system* needed to run the basic computer functions and provide the foundation that allows other software, called *applications*, to work. Applications are programs loaded onto the computer to perform functions such as word processing or more specialized tasks for broadcast operations. These days, most software is delivered from the supplier on CD-ROM discs or downloaded over the Internet.

Broadcast stations use PCs for many purposes directly associated with program production and sending to air, including processing, recording, and editing audio and video; producing computer graphics and captioning; and controlling and monitoring other systems and equipment.

Servers

Servers are powerful computers with a particular function on a *network*. They provide a centralized location for various network management and operational functions. For example, a server may run an application, such as a database, that can be accessed by many *clients*. File servers provide central storage of data for clients. Other servers manage access to the Internet, and e-mail systems, for network users. Video and audio servers are computers with particular capabilities dedicated to storing video and audio programming.

Clients

Clients are PCs connected to a network that work in conjunction with a server. In general, a client runs on its own, but it may interact with a server to send information to, or request information from, the central location.

Specialized Computers and Processors

Although PCs fill many roles in broadcasting, some applications require more power or very high reliability. In some situations, it may be possible to meet the requirement by using combinations of multiple PCs working together. In other cases, special high-end computers with different processors and/or operating systems are used.

Many items of digital broadcasting equipment incorporate computer-type processors built into the equipment itself, with instruction sets held in *nonvolatile* (permanent) memory, and which may not require an operating system or application program. Such equipment may be referred to as having *embedded systems*. The advantage of such systems is that they can often be made more reliable than general-purpose computers, and performance can be tailored to the particular application.

Storage

Files and Folders

When a computer needs to store data (e.g., programs, text, audio, video), it packages it in the form of an electronic *file*. Files come in different types, with a different suffix on their name to identify them (e.g., "doc" for Microsoft Word® documents). To organize them and make them easy to find, files are usually placed in *directories* or *folders* in the storage device being used. They can also be transferred from one computer to a storage device on another computer, over a private network or the Internet.

Disk Drives

All PCs, and many other computers, use *hard disk drives* (also known as a *hard disk* or *hard drive*) for long-term storage of programs and data. With hard disk storage, the data can be rapidly accessed, and will not be lost when the computer is turned off. Such drives can store up to hundreds of gigabytes of data on one or more spinning magnetic disks or *platters* (most hard drives have multiple platters on a single spindle). Each disk has thousands of concentric tracks that can be rapidly accessed by record/replay *heads* that move in and out over the surface of the disk. They do not actually touch the surface of the disk, because there is an air cushion between, so the disks do not wear out due to friction with the head, as happens with magnetic tape storage.

Multiple hard disk drives may be combined together in different ways to achieve much higher reliability, and/or greater capacity, than can be achieved with a single disk. One such arrangement is known as RAID (*redundant array of independent disks*). These are generally used in conjunction with servers. Large-scale disk storage systems may be in boxes separate from the associated server computers.

Other types of drives that have removable disks, such as the floppy disk, are sometimes used for data storage. Their capacity is much less than hard drives, and they are increasingly being replaced by optical disks and solid-state storage.

Tape

Where even larger amounts of data have to be stored for archive purposes, the computer (usually a server) may transfer it to special magnetic data tapes. These can store very large amounts of data for long periods with great reliability. The disadvantage is slow access to any particular piece of data, because the data is stored on a long ribbon of tape that may take a considerable time to shuttle to the required location.

Optical Disks

A more recent alternative to magnetic disk or tape data storage is *optical disc* recording, based on the *compact disc* (CD) and *digital versatile disc* (DVD) recording formats (note that optical discs are spelled with the letter c). Introduced initially as read-only memory (ROM) devices, these are available in various versions that can record to a disc once only, or that can both record and erase, for multiple uses. CDs and DVDs look similar, but CDs can hold about 700 megabytes of data, and DVDs can currently hold 4.7 gigabytes. DVDs using new technologies have been announced with capacities up to 30 gigabytes, or even more.

Solid-State

The disadvantage of all the previously mentioned storage systems is that they involve moving mechanical parts that can wear out or break. In addition, the speed of access to individual items of data is limited by the physical speed of access to the media. Both of these drawbacks are overcome with *solid-state* storage. This is memory based on silicon chips, comprising integrated circuits with millions of transistors and other components inside. Modern computers have always used solid-state RAM for their main processing functions, because it can be made with very fast access times. However, it has several drawbacks: it loses data when power is turned off, has limited capacity, and, for many years, was expensive in cost per kilobyte.

More recently, technology developments have produced solid-state memory with much larger capacities, measured in the hundreds of megabytes, or gigabytes, although with access times much slower than RAM. This type of solid-state memory is suitable for long-term mass storage because it is nonvolatile (i.e., does not lose data when the power is removed), and can be produced in a removable card or other small device form. Examples are the *flash memory* cards used for digital cameras and USB flash memory devices.

Computer Networks

LANs and WANs

Computer networks are used to connect two or more computers together to allow them to share data or resources. Frequently, one or more servers may be connected to multiple client computers on a network, and devices such as printers may also be connected for shared access. There are two main types of network: *local area networks* (LANs) and *wide area networks* (WANs). As might be expected, LANs generally operate over comparatively small areas, such as within a building, whereas WANs operate over much larger distances, spanning up to whole countries or the world.

Ethernet

By far the most common form of LAN is known as *Ethernet*. This operates over various forms of cabling: twisted pair (similar to telephone wires), coaxial cable, or fiber-optic cable, and at various data rates: 10 Mbps, 100 Mbps, 1 Gbps, and now even at 10 Gbps. Other network technologies are used for specialized purposes with LANs and for WANs.

Internet

The Internet is the worldwide, interconnected system of networks that allows computers connected to it to potentially communicate with any other connected computer or server, using the TCP/IP protocol (see following section). It consists of enormous data backbones transmitting billions of bits of data per second, with smaller distribution systems attached to the main backbones.

An *intranet* is a private network, which uses software and protocols such as those used with the Internet, but not accessible to the public. Intranets may be for local access only or may be available in multiple locations using WAN technology.

Protocols

When computers communicate over a network, or between networks, they have to use an agreed-on *protocol* (the format and operating rules) for data communication, if they are to understand each other. Numerous protocols have been established for various purposes, but the most widely used is TCP/IP (*transmission control protocol/Internet protocol*). TCP/IP is used not only for communication with the Internet but also for many other networking purposes, sometimes in conjunction with other protocols.

One of the key features of TCP/IP is that every device using it is assigned a unique *IP address*, which is used for routing messages to and from the device. Each data stream is broken into specific pieces of the data, called *packets*. Each packet has its own unique identifier containing information about where it came from and where it is destined to end up.

Switches and Routers

LANs are made up of interconnected client and server computers, frequently connected together in a "hub-and-spoke" arrangement, where each computer is connected back to a central *network switch*. This enables the computers to communicate with each other using a suitable protocol.

Routers can also serve as a switch but, in addition, they provide capabilities for secure control over what messages on the LAN are routed to which IP addresses. They allow rules to be established for which computers or servers are accessible to each other on the LAN and for connections to other networks and the Internet.

Security

A *firewall* is usually provided for a LAN to prevent unauthorized access to clients or servers from computers outside the network. The firewall may be a hardware device associated with the gateway from the outside world or may be software-based, running on a particular server or client PC.

Critical messages and data sent to systems outside of the firewall are frequently sent with *encryption*. This means they can only be decoded and understood by users with authorized computers.

Internet Streaming

Streaming is the blanket term for the distribution of audio or video, plus supplementary data, from a central distribution point over the Internet to multiple users.

Background

The technology for streaming came out of developments in several computer hardware and software fields. Apple originally created Quicktime® software to run the audio, video, and still image tasks on its Macintosh PCs. After audio cards for home personal computers became available in the early 1990s, the Real® line of software from RealNetworks arose to play audio on PCs, with streaming over telephone lines using modems; video was added later. Microsoft Corporation also added functionality to its Windows® operating system, including first the Internet Explorer World Wide Web browser and then the Windows Media Player.

In parallel with these developments, the international standards group *MPEG* (Moving Pictures Experts Group) was producing various standards for video and audio compression. The Layer 3 version of MPEG audio coding (usually known as MP3) took off as a hugely popular format for sharing and distributing audio files on the Internet, particularly for music. A version of MP3 can be used for streaming audio. Thus there are four current software standards for streaming on the Internet: *Quicktime®*, *RealMedia®*, *Windows Media®*, and (for audio only) streaming *MP3*.

Technology

Traditional broadcasting is a point-to-multipoint distribution system: one transmission site serves many thousands or millions of people in a given geographic area, with no limitations so long as they can receive an over-the-air signal. Internet streaming is somewhat different: it takes one program stream and copies the feed many times over to reach multiple customers. Each additional user requesting the program requires additional equipment and resources to be provided for distribution.

In very simple terms, the program produced by a station, or some other source, is fed into an *encoder*, which compresses the video and/or audio, and encodes it into a form that can be distributed over the Internet. One encoder must be used for each type of program stream offered: Quicktime, RealMedia, Windows Media, or MP3. Encoding may be done in two ways: (1) in hardware, where the encoding is done by a physical chip, or (2) in software, where the software does the encoding. Hardware encoders tend to be faster but require a physical chip change to update the encoding capabilities, whereas software decoders are generally slower but offer greater ability to easily update tool sets. See Chapter 15 for more information on compression.

Once a stream has been created, it must be fed to a server, which then copies the stream for each of the customers who are asking for the program. The service provider allocates a certain amount of bandwidth for the feed and provides the computer servers and data distribution equipment to get those feeds to the Internet for distribution to the end customer. If more requests for the feed are received than data space or program feeds have been created, then no more customers can be served.

Finally, the data streams must be transmitted over the open Internet. Each data stream is broken into packets and distributed using an Internet protocol as described earlier. However, unlike regular broadcasting, there is no guarantee that packets will arrive in a particular order or how long a packet will take to reach its destination. Thus, if the Internet, or the connection to the home, is under heavy load, the distribution of the packets for the audio/video stream may be disrupted. This can produce jumps in the picture or skips in the audio when a user is listening to the streaming content. The increasing use of broadband data links, such as DSL (digital subscriber lines) over telephone lines, and *cable modems* with cable television systems, is improving performance for Internet access, and this will only get better as time goes on.

The restrictions mentioned previously on how many customers can be served apply to distribution using the *unicast* model. A technique called *multicast* is also possible, which largely overcomes this restriction. It makes a single stream available to many users by replicating it within the network. However, multicast requires many changes in the way the Internet interconnections and routing are set up, and at this time not all Internet service providers support multicast.

Data Rate and Signal Quality

The data rate of the stream is governed by whether the content is audio, video, or both; it may also depend on the intended final delivery link—dial-up phone line or broadband connection. The signal quality of a given bit rate depends on both the data rate of the stream being produced and the type of encoding used. The better the encoder, the better the reproduced signal quality for a given data rate. Without exception, however, audio-only streams will be of noticeably better quality at a given bit rate than a video or video/audio stream.

For audio, the most common data rates are 8 to 24 kbps for a 28.8 kbps modem, 24 to 52 kbps for a 56 kbps modem, and 128 kbps and up for broadband data connections.

Video Standards

Unlike conventional television, computers are not single-standard devices with respect to video formats. Therefore, video via streaming does not require special equipment to reproduce video with standards different from the consumer's home country. NTSC can be viewed in 625-line countries, as can PAL and SECAM in 525-line countries.

However, even within the United States, multiple software programs may be required to view and listen to different streaming programs, because, for example, one stream may be sent using Windows Media encoding and another may be using Quicktime.

STUDIOS AND PRODUCTION FACILITIES

CHAPTER 8

Radio Studios

This chapter explains the facilities used for making radio programs, from the microphone in the studio to the link that takes the program to the transmitter. Arrangements for remote broadcasting from outside the studio are covered in Chapter 10, with program links in Chapter 11.

Types of Studios

Radio studios are special rooms where audio programs or contributions are produced for broadcasting. Apart from their technical facilities, the important thing about studios is that they are designed or adapted to be isolated from outside sounds, so there is no background noise interference with a program. Inside they have special *acoustic treatment* on the walls and ceilings to control the amount of *reverberation* (the persistence of sound due to multiple reflections after the sound source has stopped), so it does not sound as though a speaker is in a very *live* environment like a bathroom.

Local radio stations have one or more studios; studios are also located in radio network centers, production centers, and elsewhere for remote contributions. There are several varieties, depending on the type of programming and whether they are primarily for on-air use or for recording. A major distinction is whether the studio has a separate control room or whether there is a combined, *combo*, studio and control room. In a combo, the *control board* operator is also the presenter or disk jockey (DJ), who does both tasks simultaneously. The combined arrangement is extremely common for on-air studios.

A studio with a separate control room is used primarily for more complex productions. The presenters and guests, or artists (known as *talent*) are in the studio, and one or more technical operators, often with other production staff, are in the control room with the technical equipment. Usually there is a soundproof window between the two areas, for visual communications. Larger radio stations and network centers may have a studio intended for live music or other performances, with more space in both the studio and control room and more equipment.

At the other extreme, many functions for audio production, that previously needed a room full of equipment, can be done on a personal computer with a few add-on items of equipment. This advance has allowed new ways of programming and has blurred the definition of what a radio studio is. For this chapter, we will concentrate on the type of studio used by most local radio stations for on-air use, but the concepts apply elsewhere.

A small radio station may have just one studio—the on-air studio—but most will have several studios for different purposes, perhaps including a news studio and a production studio for recording programs or commercials.

Studio Operations

Traditionally, a radio station produces on-air programs with one or more live presenters and guests in a studio at the station, playing music and other program segments from various devices, and taking phone calls on the air. When needed, the on-air studio operator also selects another studio in the building (e.g., associated with a newsroom), or selects a feed from a remote source, such as a network or remote sports venue, and integrates that source into the on-air program. Depending on the station, in some cases whole programs may also come from a network or program syndication source, with a live feed or recorded medium.

Although that model still applies, the world of radio broadcasting changed greatly during the 1990s. As described below, the process is now largely automated, and in some cases, whole programs may be broadcast without the intervention of a live presenter or operator.

Automation and Live Assist

The introduction of computer hard drive audio storage equipment and computer-controlled automation for radio (described later in this chapter) changed the way most stations operate. Previously, it was largely a manual operation to play music, other material or program segments, and advertisements, from different types of tape machines, records, or CDs, interspersed with live introductions and announcements. Now most material is stored as *audio files* on a *hard disk recorder* and can be played back under the control of a *program automation* system. This may include prerecorded link announcements made by the local presenter, called *voice tracking*, and for some types of programs, the operation can effectively be run unattended for long periods.

Even when the program format, or station preferences, requires the presenter to talk live on-air (e.g., for phone-in shows), the computer can still handle the playout of all the other program segments. This mode is called *live assist*.

Remote Voice-Tracking

Remote voice-tracking takes the process one step further. In this case, a presenter or DJ at a remote location (maybe his or her home) records all of the voice segments that link a program together, and stores them as audio files on an audio workstation or computer. These files are then transferred (over the Internet, a private network, or a phone line) to the hard drive storage at the local station. The segments are identified in the automation *playlist* and are played out on-air seamlessly with the music, just as though the DJ was in the studio.

Similar techniques allow station groups to share programming among different stations, and in some cases, to control and monitor operations from centralized remote locations. This is known as *centralcasting*.

Ingest

An important operation for most radio stations is *ingest*. This involves receiving program material from outside sources and preparing it for use by the station. Feeds from networks frequently come in on *satellite links*, and live feeds may be fed to the on-air mixing console, as shown in Figure 8.1. Other material may be fed to a recording device, which these days is usually a hard disk recorder associated with an *audio workstation*, for integrating into later programs. Material may also be moved as audio files between workstations or computers within the radio station, so the ingest workstation may be separate from the on-air studio. Program segments may be produced at a different geographic location and transferred to the station over a private data network or the Internet.

Editing

At one time, most audio editing, to prepare news stories or other material for air, was done on audio tape machines by physically cutting and joining the tape. Today, almost all editing is carried out using hard disk–based audio workstations. This may be a unit dedicated for this purpose, although most types of hard disk recorders are provided with editing software.

Audio Storage

Nowadays, nearly all radio stations have much of their prerecorded music, commercials, and other material stored on computer hard drives. The continually increasing size of this type of storage and continually decreasing cost per megabyte have made this possible. Advantages of hard disk storage and playout systems, compared to previous analog systems, include the following:

- Increase in audio quality
- Much reduced wear and tear and increased reliability
- Easy automation with a single computer program on a single machine
- Automatic creation of the program log
- More efficient use of station personnel

System Considerations

Stereo or Mono

Most current audio equipment and studios are designed to work in two-channel stereo mode, and virtually all FM stations produce stereo programming. AM stations that transmit in mono only may also be set up to produce stereo programs, but they may combine the left and right channels to a mono signal at the output of the studio chain. Older stations may use only mono equipment (or stereo equipment in mono mode) with equipment interconnect wiring done with a single mono channel. When AM stations with mono studios add IBOC transmission, they will need to upgrade their studio facilities to stereo because AM IBOC is a stereo service.

Analog or Digital

The trend in radio broadcasting is to replace equipment based on analog signal processing with digital equipment. There are many advantages to this change, including those noted above for hard disk–based storage and a general increase in capabilities. However, many stations still use analog audio mixing consoles and analog interconnections, either because they have serviceable legacy installations or because they choose not to upgrade their whole facility to digital. Most items of digital audio equipment can be used as digital "islands" in an overall analog system, using analog-to-digital and digital-to-analog converters. As mentioned in Chapter 6 on this topic, every A/D and D/A conversion introduces a small quality loss, so the number of conversions backward and forward is kept to a minimum wherever possible.

Microphones at the start of the chain are inevitably analog, as are loudspeakers and headphones. In a modern facility, however, it is possible to have a DJ's voice converted to digital immediately after leaving the microphone and have it remain in digital form until after it has been fed into the transmitter. An analog FM or AM transmitter accepting digital inputs will, of course, convert the signal back to analog for transmission.

Air Chain

A station's *air chain* is the path that its on-air program material follows from the program source to the transmitter. As a rule, the arrangement for a local radio station on-air studio and air chain up to the *studio-transmitter link* (STL) will be something like the much-simplified block diagram in Figure 8.1.

Microphones and other program sources feed into an audio mixing console; the output of the console will usually pass through an *audio delay* unit and then through some sort of *distribution system* (not shown in the figure) to the *Emergency Alert System* (EAS) equipment. The output of the EAS goes through various items of *audio processing* equipment that adjust the overall sound of the station and then to the STL for sending to the transmitter.

Some of the blocks in the drawing indicate categories of equipment, not individual units, and the interconnections show the general arrangements for signal flow, not specific audio connections. In the following sections, we describe the main equipment in each of these blocks and how it all works together. Large radio stations and network centers have many more studios and other facilities than those shown here, but the types of equipment and principles of operation are much the same.

We will start with the audio mixing console, which is the heart of the studio system, and then discuss audio sources and monitoring, control systems, and, finally, the other major items of equipment and functions that make up a typical radio studio facility.

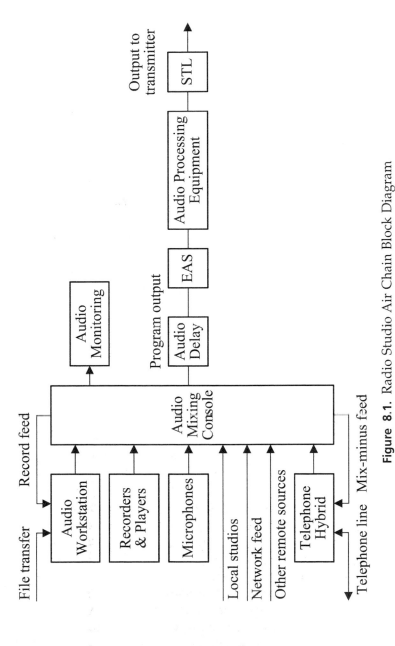

Figure 8.1. Radio Studio Air Chain Block Diagram

Audio Mixing Consoles

The audio mixing console is a device that allows several program sources to be mixed, monitored, and fed to the transmitter. An example is shown in Figure 8.2. It is often referred to as a *mixing board*, *control board*, or just a *mixer* or *board*. Both analog and digital mixing boards are widely used; both have similar facilities, although the way they process the audio inside is completely different.

Figure 8.2. Audio Mixing Board
Courtesy of Wheatstone Corporation

The mixing board has multiple signals fed into it from different program sources, such as microphones, CD players, or a hard disk recorder. It has controls that allow the operator to select each source and feed one or more simultaneously to a mixed program output called a *bus* (from "bus bar," a metal junction bar joining two or more electrical circuits). Each input has a *level* (volume) control known as a *fader* (also known as a *pot* from the name *potentiometer*, the *variable resistor* component used in most mixing boards). Faders often used to be rotary controls; today, sliding *linear faders* are universal, and the control moves in a straight line. Other input channel controls usually include a *pan-pot* (to adjust where a mono sound source appears to be located when heard on a stereo system), *balance* for stereo channels, and, in some cases, *equalization* to adjust the sound for treble, bass, and so on.

Inputs

Board inputs are of two main types: microphone and *line* inputs. Each feeds a *channel* on the mixer (not to be confused with RF channels used for transmission). Microphones have very small signal outputs and require sensitive channel inputs, which are always analog; most other equipment and distribution systems provide audio at a much higher line level. Audio levels are usually quoted in *decibels* (dB), which is a ratio compared to a standard level.

Many mixing boards, whether operating as analog or digital systems internally, are equipped to accept both analog and AES/EBU digital line level inputs.

Outputs

As well as the main program output, the board produces a *mix-minus* version of the program to send back to telephone callers. This contains the complete program but without the contributor's own audio. If their own voice is returned over the telephone, it may get fed back into the input channel again, creating a *feedback* loop. Mix-minus may also be used on occasions as a *cue feed* for other live contributions. Boards usually have other auxiliary outputs, including a feed to recording devices that may be different from the on-air program.

Monitoring

Audio monitoring is provided to allow the operator to listen to the program output or selected sources to check for program content and quality. Audio monitoring may be on high-quality loudspeakers in the control room, but, if the control room is also the studio in a combo arrangement, headphones are used to prevent interference with live microphones. Sometimes a small loudspeaker is also built into the console.

A necessary feature is *cue* or *prefade listen* (PFL) *monitoring*, which allows a source to be monitored before it is *faded up* for use.

Meters are provided to give a visual indication of the program level. This allows the operator to accurately adjust the output so it will correctly *modulate* the transmitter and not be too loud or soft. Meters may be of two types: *volume unit* (VU) and *peak program meter* (PPM), which measure the level in slightly different ways. VU meters have been used traditionally in U.S. radio stations, but modern consoles may also use peak indicators. Either sort may be actual mechanical meters or electronic displays.

Effects and Processing Units

Some types of productions need more than the basic equalization controls to change the way some audio sources sound. Audio consoles used for production and recording often have additional features, either built-in or as *outboard devices*, that provide effects such as *echo* and *reverberation*, or *pitch change* (where a voice or sound is made to sound higher or lower than it really is). Such units use *digital signal processing* (DSP) to produce the desired sound. Processing such as audio level *compression* (see section later in this chapter on audio processing equipment) may also be used, and some stations add a separate *microphone processor* for the presenter's microphone before feeding it to the console.

Operation

To illustrate the role of the mixing board in producing a live on-air radio program, consider the sequence of events that occurs when a radio announcer is talking between two program segments coming, for example, from two CD players. While the first segment is playing, the next CD is loaded and *cued* using the prefade listen monitor (i.e., the correct track is selected), and the device is left ready to go. At the end of the first segment, when the announcer wishes to talk, the first CD player is *faded down* (i.e., the fader is moved to decrease the level), and the channel switch may be turned off. Then the channel switch for the microphone input is turned on (if not already on), and the microphone is faded up, or *potted up*, and the announcer starts talking. At the same time, the channel for the next CD that will be played is potted up, although no audio is heard because the CD has not yet been started. As the announcer finishes his introduction, the channel switch for the CD player is turned on, the start button is pressed, and the music begins playing (the start action may in fact be automatic from the act of turning the channel on, or moving the fader, depending on the design). At this point, the microphone is potted down.

This is just one example of how a mixing board is used. There are many other scenarios using different input sources, which may be mixed simultaneously. Often a music piece is started while the announcer is still talking; this helps ensure that there is no silence, or *dead air*. When an announcer is talking over background music or other sounds it is called a *voice-over*.

Microphones

Microphones (often called *mics*) convert sound waves created by human voices, instruments, or other things into electrical signals. Although each model is designed a little differently, they all have generally similar design principles. Microphones are quite straight-forward and are fundamental to radio broadcasting, so we will discuss the inner workings of the two most commonly used micro-phone types: *moving coil* and *condenser*.

Moving Coil Microphone

In the moving coil (or *dynamic*) microphone, shown in Figure 8.3, a small drum-like surface called a *diaphragm* is exposed to the

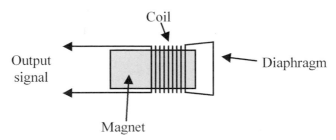

Figure 8.3. Dynamic Moving Coil Microphone Design

incoming sound pressure waves in the air and moves backward
and forward in a corresponding manner. The back of the
diaphragm is connected to a metal coil that slides up and down
over a small magnet. For reasons that are beyond the scope of this
book, the coil movement over the magnet causes an electrical signal
to be created in the wires in the coil. This signal is a reproduction,
in electrical form, of the sound waves that hit the diaphragm. The
ends of the coil are connected to the plug on the end of the microphone, and the signal can be fed from there to a mixing board.

A different type called the *ribbon microphone* operates using a
similar principle. In this case, a very thin piece of metal foil (the
ribbon) is suspended in a magnetic field, exposed to the sound
pressure wave. The movement of the ribbon causes the electrical
signal to be created in the ribbon itself.

Condenser Microphone

The condenser microphone, shown in Figure 8.4, operates using a
different principle, based on the operation of a *capacitor*. A capacitor is an electronic device with two *plates* that allow electricity to
flow from one to the other at a varying rate depending on the material between them, and their distance apart. In the condenser microphone, incoming sound waves strike a diaphragm, which forms
one plate, situated in front of a metal back plate. Together, the
diaphragm and the back plate form a capacitor. The distance
between the plates varies slightly as the diaphragm moves in accordance with the sound waves hitting it. So, if electricity is applied
to the circuit in a condenser microphone, the flow will vary, and a

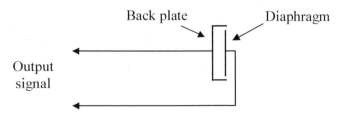

Figure 8.4. Condenser Microphone Design

signal is produced that is an electronic version of the incoming sound waves.

The main advantage of the condenser microphone is that the capacitor circuitry is much smaller and lighter than the magnet and coil used in a dynamic moving coil or ribbon microphone. For this reason, they are frequently used for small lapel or clip-on microphones (often used in television for on-camera use). Larger high-quality condenser microphones are often used for studio recordings.

Microphone Patterns

A microphone pattern refers to the directions from which it picks up sound. Microphones used in broadcasting come in four main pattern types. The *omnidirectional* picks up sound from all directions; the *cardioid* or *unidirectional* picks up sound mainly from one direction, with a little from each side; the *figure-of-eight* has a pattern like its name, and picks up sound from two opposite directions; and finally, the *shotgun* is a highly directional microphone.

A microphone may also be used in conjunction with a *parabolic dish* reflector (like a satellite receiving dish) to create an extremely sensitive directional microphone for picking up soft sounds from far distances without interference.

Loudspeakers and Headphones

We will cover loudspeakers (also known as *speakers*) and headphones next because they operate in a similar, but opposite, manner to a moving coil microphone to convert electrical signals back into sound waves.

In a speaker, an electrical signal (of a much higher level than the one that comes out of a microphone) is fed into a metal coil located in a magnetic field created by a large magnet. As shown in Figure 8.5, this metal coil is attached to a lightweight diaphragm or *cone*,

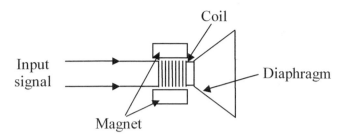

Figure 8.5. Typical Loudspeaker Design

often made of a paper-like material. The changing electrical signal in the coil causes it to move back and forth in the magnetic field, thus causing the cone to move too. The cone's motion causes the air to move, creating the sound waves, which can be heard by the human ear. These sound waves, of course, correspond to the electrical signal that is fed to the speaker through the speaker wire.

The size of the diaphragm used in a loudspeaker largely determines the range of frequencies it can reproduce well. Therefore, inside the box of a high-quality speaker system, there will always be at least two speaker units of different sizes to cover a wide audio frequency range. The speaker unit that covers the highest treble frequencies is called a *tweeter* (typically one to inches in diameter, and the one that covers medium and low frequencies is called a *woofer* (usually between about 6 and 15 inches). If there is one just for the middle frequencies, it is called a *midrange* unit. There is sometimes a special speaker in a separate box, called a *subwoofer*, to cover the extremely low bass frequencies.

Every speaker system has an associated *power amplifier* that takes a line level signal from a mixing console, or other program source, and amplifies it to the high power level needed to drive the loudspeaker units.

Headphones operate in a similar manner to loudspeakers, the main difference being that the electrical signal levels fed into them are not as strong, and, of course, the physical elements of a headphone are smaller than those of a loudspeaker.

No matter how many revolutionary changes occur in other broadcast equipment design, the basic operation of headphones, speakers, and microphones will probably remain basically unchanged. Although it is possible to convert all of the other audio signals in a broadcast facility to digital, headphones, speakers, and microphones have to retain their analog design because human voice and hearing will continue to be in analog form.

CD Players

CDs, or *compact discs*, have been for many years one of the most convenient, reliable, and highest quality forms of media for long-term storage for digital music. The digital audio on the disc is uncompressed and recorded with 44.1 kHz sampling and 16 bit resolution using *pulse code modulation* (PCM). This provides very high-quality sound reproduction. Other, more recent, recording formats such as *super audio compact disc* (SACD) allow even higher quality, but they are not widely used at this time.

A CD is reliable because the information is permanently etched, or carved, into the plastic of the disc as very small indentations or *pits*. It cannot be erased by passing through a magnetic field like the information on a recording tape can, and the only way to damage the information is to physically damage the CD by breaking or severely scratching it. Small scratches are often not a problem because CD players are able to miss a few 1s and 0s in the digital information and still accurately reconstruct the recorded music. They can do this because the digital audio data includes additional bits, added in a specially coded manner, called *forward error correction*. These enable the CD player to determine what the correct value of a missing piece of data is. An error correction system is only capable of fixing errors up to a certain point. If there are too many missing or damaged pieces of data, the error correction system will fail, and the CD will skip or stop playing.

A CD is also durable because it is not subject to any wear and tear during the playback process. A CD player reads information by shining a light (actually a laser) onto the disk and analyzing the reflections of this light that are caused by the pits recorded on it. Because there is no mechanical contact between the laser and the disc, there is no wear and tear.

Analog and Digital Connections

Most professional CD players have both analog and digital outputs. If the station's audio system is analog-based, then the analog outputs can be used to feed a signal into the mixing board. If, on the other hand, the station's audio system is digitally-based, then the digital outputs can be used.

Other CD Variants

Equipment is available for recording uncompressed audio and compressed audio files on compact discs. These devices are not widely used for radio studio operations, but they may be used for archiving audio content, to take advantage of the robust CD format.

Hard Disk Recorders and Audio Workstations

Hard Disk Recorders

Chapter 7 explained how computer hard drives can store large amounts of data as files on magnetic disks. Because digital audio is just another form of data, it follows that it can be stored in this way. Fundamentally, all such systems use a computer with an interface for the audio input and output signals (either analog or digital AES/EBU). They also typically have a separate connection that allows files to be transferred to and from other digital storage devices via a computer network, either in the same studio or across the country.

Like all computer data, the audio is stored in the form of files on the hard disk system. It may be stored uncompressed (sometimes known as *linear* recording) or, to reduce the size of the files, it may be in compressed form (see later section on audio data compression).

There are many varieties of hard disk recorders. Some are based on standard computers, with the usual keyboard, mouse, and monitor for the operator interface. Others provide front-panel controls with buttons, knobs, and indicators for specific functions; or there may be a combination of both. Most are combined with additional capabilities, as described later.

Typically, when a digital audio file is retrieved from a hard disk storage system and sent, say, to a mixing board, the playback device reads the file from the disk, formats it into an AES/EBU data stream, and sends it out through a cable to the mixing board. The mixing board receives the digital audio through an AES/EBU format input.

Digital Audio Workstations and Servers

Digital audio workstations are hard disk recorders with additional software providing functions, such as automatic ingest of audio material, editing of content, file conversion, file management, as well as basic record and replay.

Such systems may be used *off-line*, or may be associated with a production studio or on-air studio. In all cases they will typically be connected to a computer network and hence be able to share files. A system that is used to provide central storage of files is called a *file server*. Any other authorized workstation on the network can simultaneously access any file stored on the server. The file server, therefore, provides the functions of both a library and a distribution system.

Songs, commercials, newscasts, and all other types of audio segments used in a broadcast facility can be stored on a server for later recall by whatever playback device wants to use them. They can be edited, converted to different formats, and distributed to other destinations in the station or elsewhere. In addition, the server can be used for live retransmission of a digital signal as it receives it. Perhaps the most important thing about hard disk–based storage systems is that they can be easily integrated with a computer-based automation system, as described in the program automation section later in this chapter.

Digital Audio Editing

Audio editing may be carried out on general-purpose digital audio workstations or may utilize a dedicated digital editing device. In either case, program material can be selected, cut, reordered, modified, and generally prepared for transmission. Usually at least some of the functions of an audio mixing console are provided, allowing the sound to be modified and several sources to be mixed together. One big advantage, compared to traditional tape-based editing, is the ability to access all program segments with *random access* instantly from hard disk storage, and also to go back and revise edits already made early in the program without affecting later edits. This *random access* feature allows *nonlinear editing*, which is in sharp contrast to having to shuttle a tape backward and forward to locate a particular program segment.

Audio Data Compression

The digital bit rate from a CD player is more than 1.4 megabits per second. This means that long segments of music or other programs will require very large files when recorded on a hard disk.

A technique called *audio data compression,* based on *perceptual coding,* may be used to reduce the amount of data needed to transport or store digital audio. Note that this type of compression has nothing to do with the audio level compression that takes place in audio processing (see later sections in this chapter). There are many different audio compression systems. The most commonly used in radio are MPEG-1 layers 1 and 2, MPEG layer 3 (usually known as MP3), and AC-2. More recent systems include MPEG AAC

(*Advanced Audio Coding*), and the HDC system used in IBOC digital radio. There is also the AC-3 system widely used in digital television. The same general psycho-acoustical principles apply for most audio compression systems, although there are many differences in implementation; for a general description see Chapter 15 under Audio Compression on page 247.

The continual increase in the size of hard drives, coupled with reductions in cost, has reduced the need for compression for audio storage. Therefore, some stations now use uncompressed audio for music storage, which increases the quality somewhat and may have other advantages (see the later section on studios for IBOC transmission).

Radio Program Automation

An automation system replaces one or more persons, to perform repetitive tasks according to preprogrammed rules and at particular times. In the case of an on-air radio station, the program automation system is a software program that runs on a computer, usually associated with the on-air studio. The basic task is to start program segments in the right order and at the right times. Most automation systems can start external devices, such as CD players or tape machines, using remote control contacts, but the real advantages come when the program material is stored as audio files on a hard disk storage system.

It is usual for the automation system to run on the same computer as a digital audio workstation. It is then straightforward for the whole process of program scheduling and audio playout to be combined together.

If live presenter links are not required, it is therefore possible, with a full-featured audio workstation, to produce and send out a complete program without using an audio mixing console at all. Most stations, however, need the flexibility that a traditional mixing console provides and usually use both systems together, with the digital audio workstation feeding an input of the mixing console.

Scheduling and Other Functions

Planning the program schedule and preparing the *playlist* for the on-air program may be carried out within a suite of programs associated with the automation system. These will be accessible from various computers on the network and will often include interfaces to other functions, such as the *traffic system*, which is used for managing the sale of advertising time, and *asset management*, which keeps track of program material and the rights to use it.

Digital Record/Playback Devices

Digital Cart

Digital cart machines provide all the functionality of a traditional analog tape cartridge machine (see later section) but use hard disk storage to provide greatly enhanced capabilities. They have simple front-panel controls for easy recording, selection, and playback of material. Usually, they are connected to a network to access commercials, promos, or other items produced elsewhere, but most also have some built-in editing facilities. Such devices are typically used for live shows, where there is not time to schedule all the segments with the automation system.

A variant of the digital cart provides a type of control panel known as a *shot box*, with many individual buttons. In this device, hundreds or thousands of individual audio segments (e.g., sound effects, or any short program segment) can be rapidly assigned to individual buttons and recalled and played instantly.

Solid-State Recorder

The advent of inexpensive, large-capacity, solid-state *flash memory* cards has enabled a new generation of digital recording devices. Available in both battery-powered portable versions and fixed studio versions, these machines combine the capabilities of digital MiniDisc and analog cassette recorders with the advantage of audio files that are compatible with hard disk recording systems. They have analog and digital audio input and output connections, and are able to connect to a computer or audio workstation for file transfer. Thus, they can be used as stand-alone record/replay devices or as acquisition devices for a file server.

MiniDisc Recorder

The *MiniDisc* format records about 80 minutes (up to five hours in a long-play mode) of stereo audio on a small, removable magneto-optical disc. The record head moves over the surface of the disc, recording a track as the disc rotates, using a proprietary audio data compression format called ATRAC (adaptive transform acoustic coding). The recording system uses a laser and a magnet, where the laser within the drive heats the magnetic surface to a high enough temperature to allow the surface of the disc to be modified via a magnet. For replay, data is read from the disc with a laser of less intensity. The format is robust and suitable for both field and studio use. It provides random access for rapid location of program tracks, and many machines contain some electronic editing features. Portable MiniDisc recorders largely replaced cassette tape recorders for newsgathering and location recording, and most radio studios include a studio version for playback. However, MiniDisc recorders have, to some extent, been superseded by solid-state recorders.

Digital Audio Tape (DAT) Recorder

The digital audio tape (DAT or R-DAT) recorder offers major advantages over analog tape, because its underlying digital technology enables it to record and play back audio with negligible noise and other degradations.

The DAT format uses 4 millimeter magnetic tape housed in a cassette. The tape head is mounted on a rotating drum (hence the R in R-DAT) and uses *helical scan* as used with television recording systems. The standard recording time is up to two hours on one tape, but a long-play mode can allow up to six hours at lower quality. The digital audio signal is uncompressed PCM, with alternative sampling rates of 32 kHz, 44.1 kHz, and 48 kHz, and 12 or 16 bit resolution.

One disadvantage of DAT compared to open-reel analog recorders is that it is impossible to edit the tape using cut and splice techniques. Also, while digital audio tape offers greatly improved audio quality, it is still subject to some of the same mechanical problems, including malfunctions with the tape transport mechanism, and wear and tear with the tape, which can cause signal *dropout* and audio interruption or degradation.

Analog Devices

At one time, analog record turntables and audio tape recorders were the mainstay of broadcasting. To give a historical perspective, we are including a brief summary of the main types. Examples of these machines may still be found in most radio stations, although nowadays they are used mainly for playing archive material and transferring (*dubbing*) it to modern digital media.

Analog Turntable

Before the days of CDs, consumer music was for many years distributed on vinyl disks known simply as *records*. A 7 inch disk, rotating at 45 revolutions per minute (rpm), holds up to about 5 minutes of audio per side. A 12 inch *long-playing record*, rotating at 33 1/3 rpm, holds up to about 30 minutes of audio per side.

On a record, the audio signal is carried mechanically as variations in the width and height of a very fine spiral groove pressed into the surface of the disk. The two channels of a stereo recording are coded and carried on opposite sides of the same groove. To play such a record, it is placed on a rotating turntable. A diamond *stylus*, underneath a *pickup cartridge* attached to the end of a pivoted *tone arm*, is placed in the groove, and the variations in the groove cause the stylus to vibrate as the disk rotates. The pickup cartridge turns the vibrations into left and right electrical audio signals (usually using magnetic detection, like a moving coil microphone).

Cart Machine

Cart (short for "cartridge") machines, using a cartridge with an endless loop of 1/4 inch tape inside, were useful for playing short program segments, such as commercials, fillers, and so on. Their big advantages were simple push-button controls, nearly instant start, and the use of *cue tones*. These inaudible tones identified the beginning and end of a recording, so the machine could cue itself, and one machine could trigger another to start, for an automated sequence (e.g., for a commercial break).

Reel-to-Reel

Reel-to-reel recorders (also called *open-reel*), because of their long lengths of easily accessible 1/4 inch recording tape, were most useful for recording and playing back long programs and for editing program material by actually cutting and splicing the tape. The system records stereo channels using two parallel tracks on the tape. Various tape speeds are used, the highest normally being 15 inches per second, which provides high quality. Long-play versions, using very low tape speeds, were often used for logging and archive purposes. Versions of this type of recorder, with tape up to 2 inches wide, are still used for multitrack music recording, although not widely used in radio studios.

Cassette

Portable *cassette* recorders use 1/8 inch tape in a plastic cassette, identical to that still used by some consumers for music today. Because of their compact size, these machines were useful for recording audio in the field, such as news interviews, and they may still occasionally be used for that purpose. Fixed versions are used to play the cassettes back in the studio and are still frequently installed in studio control rooms to accommodate material that may arrive in this format.

Noise Reduction

One of the drawbacks of analog audio tape is the well-known *tape hiss* noise that all analog tape recordings have to a greater or lesser extent. High-quality open-reel machines running at higher tape speeds, and with sophisticated tape coating materials, are able to reduce this noise considerably, but slower-speed machines, particularly cassette recorders, suffer from it quite badly. The difference between the audio signal level and the hiss, or other noise on the tape, is called the *signal-to-noise ratio*. The larger the signal-to-noise ratio, the better the recording sounds. A low S/N ratio will result in a recording that sounds "hissy."

To help overcome the tape noise problem, Dolby Laboratories developed a system of *noise reduction* for analog tape. Dolby® noise-reduction technology is a sophisticated form of *equalization*. During recording, the professional *Dolby A* system uses amplification of low-level sounds in many narrow frequency ranges over the entire audio range. During playback, the same sounds are suppressed back to their original level, which simultaneously reduces the noise introduced by the tape. Dolby B circuitry is a less complex—and therefore less expensive—version, which is still widely used for prerecorded music cassettes. It operates primarily at higher frequencies. Dolby C is an enhanced version of Dolby B, but it is not much used. Dolby noise reduction and processing is widely adopted in the motion picture industry and the Dolby system is used for many film sound tracks.

Telephone Hybrids

The interface to an analog telephone line to be used on-air requires a device called a *telephone hybrid*. This piece of equipment converts incoming audio from the phone line into a line level signal that can be fed into a mixing board. It also converts a line level signal coming out of a mixing board into an audio signal that can be fed over the phone line back to the caller.

The hybrid allows the caller to be heard on air, and the show host to hear the caller without having to pick up a telephone handset. At the same time, it allows the caller to hear the talk show host and the rest of the program. It ensures that only the caller's voice is of telephone quality, while the show host's voice remains of broadcast quality.

Remote Sources

Most stations receive at least some programming, including news, weather, sportscasts, or network programming, from remote sources. These will appear as inputs on the mixing console, either direct or via an *audio routing switcher* (see later section). These remote contributions are often distributed by *satellite link* if they are coming from a network or organization distributing to multiple stations. A local station, receiving remote broadcasts and news reports from the field, will usually use either *remote pickup units* (RPUs) or telephone lines as links. The *terminal equipment* for such links is usually in the master control room, and the audio is fed from there to the mixing console. See Chapter 11 for more information on links.

When working with station staff in the field, a mix-minus feed is often sent to the contributor over a *return channel* as a *cue feed*, as for a telephone contribution. Where this is not possible, the remote site may monitor the station off-air signal for cue information.

Audio Delay Units

The *audio delay unit* (also known as the *profanity delay*) follows the audio console and usually provides between five and ten seconds of audio storage and delay. It is used for live programming, where it is possible that a contributor (perhaps a telephone caller) may say something unacceptable on the air. If that happens, the operator can press a button that "dumps" the offending words before they leave the delay unit heading for the transmitter.

Delay units in use today use digital circuitry, although their input and output interfaces may be either analog or digital.

Emergency Alert System

The Emergency Alert System (EAS) is the communications network designed by the federal government to allow the President to speak to the entire nation in the event of a national emergency. Although the primary function of the EAS is for national alerts, it has a secondary purpose—providing state and local officials with a means of alerting local communities about local emergencies such as severe weather, chemical leaks, fires, and so on.

From an engineering standpoint, the way EAS operates is relatively simple. As shown in Figure 8.6, the EAS encoder/decoder is installed in a station's air chain so it can interrupt the flow of normal programming to the transmitter, in order to insert an emergency message.

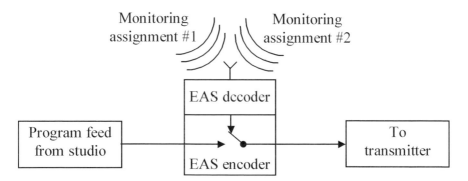

Figure 8.6. EAS Equipment in a Radio Station Air Chain

The EAS decoder constantly monitors the transmissions from at least the two input sources to which it has been assigned, for a special digital code signifying an alert of a particular type. The two sources include other broadcast stations, but many stations also monitor National Oceanic and Atmospheric Administration (NOAA) weather service broadcasts. Having two sources helps ensure that the decoder will still receive an alert message if one of its monitoring assignments happens to be off the air.

If an alert is received by the EAS decoder, of a type that the rules for the station determine should be passed on, then the EAS encoder will break into the station's air chain and transmit the alert in place of the regular programming. Encoders can be programmed to do this automatically. Alternatively, they may be set up to automatically record the alert message for later broadcast and require a person to manually interrupt the station's programming for the EAS message.

Testing of the EAS national distribution is conducted weekly, and also requires over-the-air transmissions with test announcements once per month.

Audio Processing Equipment

Reasons for Processing

One purpose of audio processing equipment is to create a "signature sound" for the radio station, or at least to take the audio that comes from the microphone, CD player, or other source and enhance it to make it sound better when heard on a radio at home or in the car. The other purpose is to prevent signals that are too high in amplitude from being sent to the transmitter. Some stations employ several different pieces of equipment to carry out a lot of processing if they are looking for a particular "sound". Other stations do less processing and might only have a single audio processor. Processing requirements for AM stations are very different from FM due to the restricted audio bandwidth and higher noise level of AM stations. IBOC channels, with their different characteristics, have another set of processing requirements.

From an engineering standpoint, the main purpose of audio processing is to maintain the level of energy in the station's audio to within a specified range, and to prevent overmodulation of the transmitter. Usually, the processing is done in discrete audio frequency bands throughout the range of the audio signal. One way to help understand how this process works is to imagine an *equalizer*, similar to one you might have on your home stereo or car radio. An equalizer is designed to amplify, or suppress, the signal level within particular portions of the audio frequency range. Increasing the level of higher-frequency signals will make the audio have more treble, and increasing the level of lower-frequency signals will make the audio have more bass. What is different with broadcast processing is that the amount of equalization performed is dynamic (i.e., it changes with time), and it is usually a function of the program content. The next few sections provide a lot more detail on processing and how it is carried out. If you feel this is more than you need to know, just skip to the section on Signal Distribution on page 109.

Loudness

Let's consider an example of this process for adjusting the program sound. We will assume that the processor has three different frequency bands: low (bass), midrange, and high (treble). Let's say that the station using this equipment wants the on-air signal to have as high a level (volume) as possible in all three bands. In this situation, the processor will be set to increase the signal level in each band. If a station, perhaps, wants a more bass-heavy sound, it would increase the low-frequency band, or for good speech clarity, increase the midrange band.

In a home stereo system, increasing the signal level is very simple: the level (volume) control across the whole frequency band is simply turned up. In a broadcast audio processing system, however, things are a bit more complicated, largely because FCC rules limit the *modulation,* and therefore the level (volume), of the transmitted audio.

The level of the transmitted audio is very important. The primary reason why most radio stations use audio processing is to increase the *loudness* of their signals. Loudness is not quite the same as volume; it takes account of the frequency makeup of the audio signal and also its *dynamic range* (the range of levels from small to large). Many broadcasters believe that a signal, which sounds louder, will be perceived by the listener as being stronger and, therefore, better. It will usually be more audible in environments with background noise, such as in a car. Original recordings and other program material often have a wide dynamic range (i.e., some parts of the program have much higher amplitude than other parts). The secret to making a broadcast station sound loud is to increase the level of the softer portions of the program material, while decreasing the level of the louder portions (i.e., to compress the audio). The aim is to keep the output level sent to the transmitter as constant as possible. This enables the station to remain in compliance with the FCC's modulation limits for the transmitted signal.

Maintaining Loudness and Controlling Modulation

The FCC sets a maximum limit on modulation for two main reasons: (1) to help ensure that broadcaster's signals do not interfere with one another, and (2) to maintain a reasonably similar audio level from all stations, providing a stable listening environment for the audience. Modulation increases and decreases with the level of a station's program material. The stronger the program material is when it is fed into the transmitter's exciter, the greater the modulation level.

Several pieces of equipment are typically used to make a radio station's signal sound as loud as possible, while maintaining modulation within permitted limits: equalizers, compressors/expanders, limiters, and clippers. They are generally installed in a station's air chain in the order of the boxes shown in Figure 8.7.

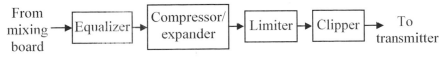

Figure 8.7. Audio Processing Equipment in a Typical Air Chain

Although shown as separate items of equipment in the figure, the equalization and compression/expansion functions are often performed by the same unit. Equalization is needed to perform the boosting or suppression of the signal level over the appropriate frequency ranges. Compression ensures that the boosted signal does not exceed the FCC modulation limit. Expansion is needed to ensure that low-level (quiet) signals, such as background noise and electronic hiss, are suppressed and not amplified to the point that they become annoying. Limiting is needed to further suppress any peaks in the signal that still exceed the FCC modulation limit after compression, and clipping "chops off" any excessive peaks that make it out of the limiter.

Let's look at some diagrams that illustrate what happens during each step in the process.

Equalization, Compression/Expansion

Figure 8.8 illustrates the signal level of an unprocessed audio signal across all audio frequencies. The obvious way to increase the loudness of this signal is simply to increase the signal level (turn up the volume) in the desired frequency bands using an equalizer. The

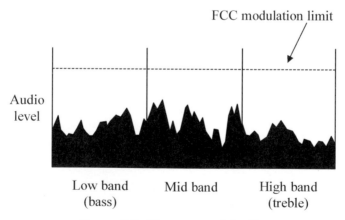

Figure 8.8. Unprocessed Audio

signal that results from this action when all frequencies are increased equally is illustrated in Figure 8.9. Alternatively, a station that is interested in having more bass in its signal, for example, would increase the lower frequencies to a greater degree than the higher frequencies.

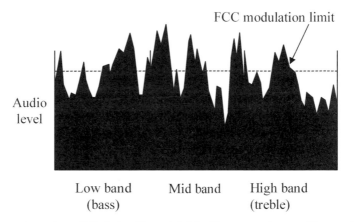

Figure 8.9. Amplified Audio with No Compression or Expansion

Figure 8.9 shows that simply raising the level produces a major problem for a radio station—overmodulation. All of the signal above the dashed "FCC modulation limit" line in Figure 8.9 will cause the radio station's signal to exceed the limit specified by the FCC. This overmodulation might cause the station's signal to interfere with the signals from other broadcast stations. Another, somewhat more subtle, problem caused by simply raising the level of the entire signal is the amplification of lower-level (softer) signals that, in many cases, are likely to be just background noise or electronic hiss. The "valleys" in the signal shown in the figure are the areas where this might be a problem.

In order to correct these two problems, the station must perform both compression and expansion of its audio. Specifically, it must use compression to reduce the audio signal's level at those points where it exceeds the FCC's modulation limit, and it must use expansion to decrease the signal's level at those points where the signal is so low that it is likely to contain only background noise or electronic hiss. An illustration of where compression and expansion might be used is provided in Figure 8.10.

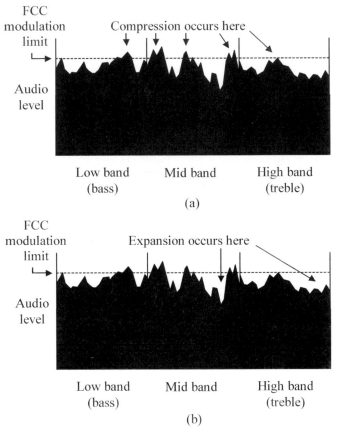

Figure 8.10. Amplified (Louder) Audio with Compression and Expansion

Broadcast processing equipment differs from an equalizer found in some home stereo systems, because the broadcast equipment is able to automatically adjust the amount of compression (and other processing) based on the program material. A home equalizer will always suppress a signal at, for example, 1 kHz (if it is set to do so), whereas a broadcast processor will suppress a signal at 1 kHz only if the signal is above the "threshold of compression" to which it is set. Similarly, the "threshold of expansion" is the signal level below which the expander will reduce the signal.

Limiting and Clipping

In addition to equalizers, compressors, and expanders, two other processing devices are commonly found in broadcast audio chains: limiters and clippers. These both essentially compress the audio signal to varying degrees, but much more aggressively than a "plain" compressor.

A limiter is typically used to take the peaks that still exist in a signal after compression and knock them down further. This is sometimes necessary when, after compression, a signal still has peaks in it that are high enough to result in overmodulation and a violation of FCC rules. A *clipper* is generally used as a last resort to "chop off" any remaining excessive peaks after the signal has passed through both the compressor and the limiter. If not used correctly, a clipper can cause severe distortion to a signal, because it literally clips the peaks off—it does not "softly adjust" the level like the compressor and limiter—so it must be used with care.

Although the configuration of processing equipment described previously is typical, it should be noted that audio processing is as much an art as it is an engineering science. Equalizers, compressors, expanders, limiters, and clippers can be used in a variety of configurations and locations in the broadcast chain. This type of equipment is available using either analog or digital processing.

Signal Distribution

Audio Interconnections

The way audio signals are transported between different items of equipment, and between different areas in a radio facility, depends largely on whether the signals are analog or digital. Analog signals use a type of cabling called *twisted pair* (two wires twisted together), which may run in individual cables or large *multicore* cables with many signals. Such cables frequently have a metal *shield* wrapped around the inner wires to keep out interference. AES/EBU digital audio signals may use similar twisted pair cabling, or alternatively may be carried on *CAT-5* cabling, as used for computer data net-

works, or on *coaxial cable* (with a single center conductor sur-
rounded by an outer conductor that acts both as a shield and the
second conductor for the program signal). For very long runs, up
to many miles, audio signals may be carried over *fiber-optic* cables.

Patch Panel

To allow signals to be checked at different locations in the distribution system, and for sources and destinations to be *cross-plugged*,
cabling is often brought to a *patch panel*. This is an array of special
sockets where a *patch cord* (a short cable with a *jack plug* on each
end) can be plugged into one circuit source, and the other end is
then plugged into a particular destination as required.

Routing Switcher

Larger stations will often use an electronic *audio routing switcher*
(also known as a *router* or *matrix*) to supplement or replace the
patch panels. This unit takes inputs from multiple sources and
allows each one to be connected to one or more destinations. Each
output may be connected to any one of the inputs at any given time.
The component in the switcher that allows an input to be connected
to an output is called a *crosspoint*. Control of the switcher may be
from a local panel (usually in the master control room) or there may
be one or more remote control panels at particular destinations.
Such routers may be of virtually any size, from a few sources and
destinations to many hundreds on inputs and outputs. Figure 8.11
shows the general arrangement. Different types of routing switchers are used for analog and digital signals.

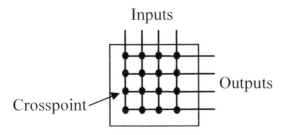

Figure 8.11. Routing Switcher Configuration

One important feature of a routing switcher is its ability to route many different signals to a particular place—such as an input channel on a mixing board—through only one connection. As an example, a station may have many remote sources that it uses at different times, but a particular studio may only need to use one or two at any given time. So, instead of wiring all of the remote sources directly to the studio mixing board (which would take up numerous input channels there), they are connected as inputs on the routing switcher. In this case, perhaps two routing switcher outputs are connected to the studio mixing board inputs. Then, by using the routing switcher control panel to select the source required, the operator has access to all of the remote sources he or she may require, but taking up only two of the mixing board inputs.

Distribution Amplifier

A routing switcher allows signals to be sent to multiple destinations on a selectable basis, but sometimes a fixed distribution of one source may be required to be sent to many destinations simultaneously. In that case, a *distribution amplifier* (often referred to as a DA) is used. This small piece of equipment takes one input and produces many outputs of the same signal. It has two other features: one is that the output signals are isolated from each other, so a fault (maybe a short) on a cable going to one destination will not affect the signal to another destination. The other is that the level of the signal can be raised if necessary to compensate for losses in a long cable run. Different types of DAs are used for analog and digital signals and either type may incorporate a *cable equalizer*, which adjusts the frequency response of the amplifier to compensate for the high frequency loss of the cable.

Ancillary Systems

Clocks and Timers

Radio stations must have accurate time for scheduling and live announcements. The clock system usually provides slave clocks with second hands, or digital displays, in all studios and control rooms. These are driven from a highly accurate *master clock* in master control. The master clock also provides accurate time to the program automation system and other computer systems that need it. These days the master clock may be synchronized automatically with *global positioning system* (GPS) signals received from satellites. Otherwise, it may get time updates from standard time references transmitted over the air or received over a phone line.

Digital *timers* are used by operators, producers, and announcers to accurately time program segments, often with a time countdown to indicate how long to go to the next event.

Intercom and Talkback

Communication is frequently required between operators and talent in different control rooms and studios. An *intercom* system usually covers all technical areas in the facility and allows anyone to talk to anyone else. A *talkback* system usually works between specific areas (e.g., a control room and studio). For instance, it allows a control room operator or producer to talk to talent in the studio. Where talkback and intercom have loudspeakers in a studio with microphones that may be used on-air, the loudspeaker is automatically *muted* whenever a microphone is in use and *live*.

On-Air Lights and Cue Lights

On-air lights warn people in the vicinity of or inside a studio that a broadcast is in progress. Depending on the system design, the lights may be on whenever the studio is in use or they may be turned on only when a microphone is actually live.

Cue lights are used to signal to talent in a studio when to start or stop speaking. The controls are in the control room and the lights can be turned on or flashed by an operator or producer.

Radio Master Control

Somewhere in a radio facility will be the *master control*. This is the central technical control point, where the equipment associated with program feeds in and out of the facility is monitored and managed and the station off-air program signal is monitored. Equipment for the EAS, audio processing, routing, distribution, and other ancillary functions, and the *transmitter remote controls*, will also usually be located here. In a small station, master control may be part of the on-air studio, but otherwise it will be a separate technical area.

Other Considerations and Capabilities

Studios for IBOC Transmission

Studio systems, whether analog or digital, that produce high-quality stereo programming for an analog service are usually acceptable for digital IBOC transmission. However, IBOC relies on heavy audio data compression called HDC (see page 216), carried out when the signal is processed at the transmitter site. This requires care to be taken with how the audio is handled at the studio.

One consideration is that some hard disk recording systems, and other digital recorders, use audio compression to save space on the recording medium. This may produce very good audio quality when transmitted on an analog AM or FM station. However, if the *compression algorithm* used in the recorder is incompatible with HDC, then *compression artifacts* (distortions of various sorts) may result in the IBOC transmission, due to interaction between HDC and the signal received from the recorder codec. To avoid this, the audio chain at the studios should preferably not use any compression, or if it does, it must be kept at a light level and should be compatible with HDC.

IBOC processing uses a 44.1 kHz sampling frequency (see the digital audio section in Chapter 6), as standardized for compact discs. However, most professional digital studio equipment uses 48 kHz. For maximum compatibility, studios for IBOC should be designed to use 44.1 kHz sampling throughout, or 48 kHz throughout (with conversion to 44.1 kHz at the transmitter). Failing that, the number of conversions between different sampling rates should be kept to a minimum.

If a single STL (see Chapter 11) is used to carry the left and right stereo program to the analog and IBOC transmitters, the separate audio processing equipment for each service must be located at the transmitter site, after the feeds have been split. If separate STLs are used for the analog and digital signals, the audio processors can be at either the studio or transmitter ends of the link.

Internet Streaming

When a broadcaster wishes to send programming to the Internet, the audio bitstream is either produced by an encoder at the station, taking a feed from the same distribution that feeds the transmitter, or from a second feed that allows for the dropping or adding of Internet-specific programming and advertisements. Alternatively, the audio feed may be sent to a third-party organization that takes care of all the details of audio encoding, provision of servers, and interfacing to the Internet.

Multitrack and Multichannel Systems

Most radio stations work with two-channel stereo sound. However, studios used for recording in the music business have *multitrack* capabilities. This allows individual parts of a performance to be recorded separately, with 16, 24, or more separate tracks on the mixing console and recorders. This makes it easier to control and adjust the final *mixdown* to a stereo *master* recording at a later time. Some radio stations have similar facilities for large production music studios.

Somewhat different from multitrack systems are multichannel facilities for *surround sound*, which is becoming increasingly common in production for digital television. The IBOC digital radio system has the possibility of carrying surround sound, so this is something that radio stations may perhaps wish to add in the future.

Advanced Systems

The previous system and equipment descriptions start from an assumption of fairly conventional interconnection arrangements. However, the latest generation of studio equipment coming from some manufacturers allows for different system architectures. It is now possible for audio mixing, switching, and processing equipment to be largely centralized and functions such as mixing board control surfaces to be remote from where the actual audio signals are. This arrangement can greatly reduce the amount of audio wiring in a large plant and allows very flexible arrangements for system design and operations. Further details are outside the scope of this book.

CHAPTER 9

Television Studios

This chapter explains the facilities used for making television programs, from the cameras and microphones in the studio to the link that takes the program to the transmitter. We will cover the major parts of the production and distribution chain, and then discuss particular studio systems and equipment.

Station and Network Operations

In the United States, each local broadcast TV channel comes from a station with a transmitter near the community of license, almost always with a studio facility in the city area. Although some programming (e.g., local news) is usually produced in studios at the station, many programs actually come from a network, which sends its programs to many stations around the country from a *network release center*, via a *network distribution* system. Figure 9.1 is a typical, but much-simplified, television network block diagram showing the end-to-end signal flow. Note that arrangements outside the United States are frequently different from this architecture, because having multiple local broadcast stations affiliated with a network is not the norm.

As indicated in the figure, some network programs may be produced in studios at the network center, but many come from *production* and *postproduction* centers elsewhere. Delivery of finished programs to the network may be via an audio/video feed, as a recorded program on tape, or as an electronic file.

The postproduction process, where recorded material is edited and assembled into finished programs, may take place at the same

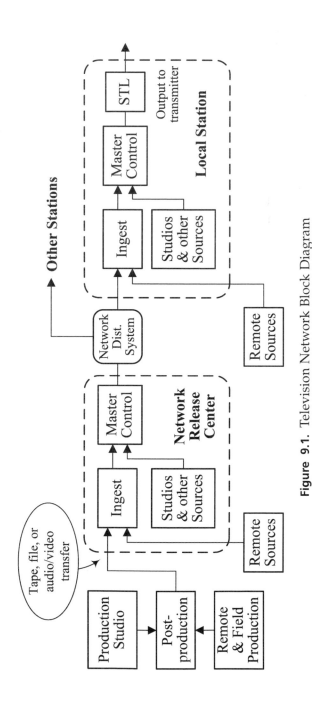

Figure 9.1. Television Network Block Diagram

location as the production studio or may be in a separate specialized *post-house*. Network centers and local stations also have editing and postproduction systems for news and other programming.

Studio and postproduction equipment and systems are usually similar, whichever part of the system they happen to be located in. Master control playout facilities at the network center and local stations also have many features in common. The major items of equipment and functionality for all these systems are described in the sections that follow, while arrangements for remote broadcasting from outside the studio are covered in Chapter 10, with program links in Chapter 11.

Centralcasting

In the *centralcasting* arrangement, station group owners may produce or originate programming (particularly news) at a central location and distribute it to their individual stations at remote locations. The operation may go further than this, and for some, or all, of the day the entire program schedule may originate at the central location and be distributed to the local station only for transmission. This potentially reduces the amount of equipment and staff needed at each station, at the expense of possibly reducing the local flavor of the station programming.

Types of Studios

As with radio, television studios are special rooms or spaces in which programs are produced for broadcasting, this time with both sound and pictures. Studios at local stations, network centers, or production centers vary considerably in size and overall capabilities, but most are based on the same principles.

Studios may range in size from small rooms, with one or two cameras for simple presentations, to big production studios of 10,000 square feet or more, with many cameras and space for complex shows. The larger studios are usually associated with production centers, where they are sometimes referred to as *sound stages*, from the term used in the film industry for a studio where movies with sound are shot. A local television station usually has a midsize studio for live news and weather presentations, and may also have other studios for recording special productions or commercials. Often, one studio may be arranged with several sets in different areas, which can be used for different parts of a program, or even for different programs.

Unlike radio, the on-air control point for television broadcasting, whether at a network release center or a local station, is not associated with a studio but is a separate *master control room* or area.

Studio Characteristics

A television studio obviously has to be large enough to accommodate all the talent and the *set* (or sets)—the area with furniture and a *backdrop* where the action takes place. It also needs enough space for the number of cameras used to shoot the action, with space to move around the studio floor.

As with radio studios, television studios are usually designed or adapted to be isolated from outside sounds, and they are fitted with *acoustic treatment* to control the amount of *reverberation*. Soundproof doors provide access for talent and production staff. In addition, very large soundproof scenery doors are provided to allow scenery and sets to be brought in and out from adjacent storage and construction areas. Except for simple studios with fixed cameras, the floor has to be hard and flat, to allow cameras mounted on *pedestals* to be moved smoothly.

Television studios have one or more associated control rooms, where the technical operators, production staff, and some of the technical equipment are located. Sometimes, but not always, there is a soundproof window between the studio and the control room to allow production staff a direct view of the action in the studio.

So that the studio lights stay out of view of the cameras, they have to be hung at a high level. The *lighting grid*, from which the light fittings are suspended, must be high enough, perhaps up to 30 feet or more from the floor in a large studio, so high ceilings are necessary. A high-level track is usually provided around the edge of the studio to hang large curtains as backdrops for sets. A light-colored background, known as a *cyclorama* (either a curtain or a hard surface), may be provided with special lighting, so decorative colored backgrounds can be produced by selecting suitable light settings.

Frequently, the studio has extra height above the lighting grid to accommodate large air-conditioning ducts, which bring in cold air and remove the heat produced by the studio lighting. They have to be large so that the air passing through the vents can be kept at low velocity, thus avoiding the sound of rushing air being picked up by microphones. This type of low-noise air-conditioning is also needed in radio studios, but is much easier to achieve there, because the lighting heat loads are far lower and less cold air is needed.

Studio Lighting

It is necessary to illuminate sets and talent with sufficient light for the cameras to produce good pictures. The light must be at a consistent *color temperature*—it is bad to mix lights that have a high color temperature (tending toward blue, like midday daylight or some types of fluorescent lights) with those that have a low color temperature (tending toward yellow or red, like a regular household light bulb, or daylight at sunset). Lights also need to be shone in the right places and directions to achieve the desired artistic effects.

Light Fixtures and Fittings

Special lighting fittings, correctly known as *luminaires*, are suspended from an overhead lighting grid, often with *telescopic hangers*, *pantographs*, or *lighting hoists* or *battens*. Some may be mounted on tripods. *Soft lights* are used for diffused lighting to reduce shadows, and *spotlights* of various types provide lighting with more control of direction, and harder shadows. *Cyclorama lights* and *ground rows* are used to evenly illuminate areas of back-drop. Light fittings can be fitted with colored filters, known as *gels*, to add color or *scrims* to diffuse the light. Spots can have *barn doors* and *flags*, which are movable metal shields to restrict where the light falls.

The actual light source (bulbs or tubes) may be of several different kinds, both *incandescent* (with a filament) and *discharge* (without a filament), with different color temperatures and various advantages and disadvantages for each. Power may range from a few hundred watts up to 10 kilowatts (kW) for a single lamp. Most studio lights are fed from *dimmers* controlled from a *lighting console*, which is usually in the *vision control* room or area.

Studio Control Rooms

One or more studio control rooms house staff and equipment for the following:

- Lighting control
- Vision (camera) control
- Sound control
- Production control

Depending on the overall design and space available, these may be separate control rooms or they may be combined together in one area. It is common for the sound control room to be separate, so that loud sound levels do not distract other production staff.

The lighting control area houses the lighting console with memories for different settings of light intensities, cross-fades, and so on. The *lighting director* uses the lighting console to remotely control each lamp in the studio to achieve the desired effect. The studio action is viewed on *picture monitors* in the control room, showing the output of each camera. The *vision engineer* also looks at the picture monitors and the *waveform monitors* for each camera, and adjusts remote camera controls to produce good-looking pictures that are also technically correct.

The audio control room or area has an audio mixing console and associated equipment, where the sound supervisor is responsible for producing the audio mix from the studio microphones and other sound sources.

Production control contains one or more desks with control panels for the *video switcher*, operated by the *technical director*, and other equipment such as a *character generator* and *graphics system*. This is also where the producer and other production staff sit. A bank of picture monitors, often mounted in a *monitor wall*, shows the output of each studio camera and other video sources, with two larger monitors for the Program and Preview outputs.

Most other equipment related to the studio is usually mounted in equipment racks in an *apparatus room* or *central technical area*.

System Considerations

It will be apparent from the previous description that having to deal with vision as well as sound produces a major increase in complexity for a television studio. This extends all the way through the system. As with radio, some basic considerations apply to all television systems, including the following points.

Standard or High Definition

Most prime-time network programming is produced and distributed in high definition (HD) format although, at the time of writing this book, there is also still significant production of standard definition (SD) material. During the transition to all-DTV broadcasting, local TV stations feed both analog NTSC and digital ATSC transmitters. Studio facilities, therefore, have to accommodate an SD program feed for the NTSC channel, and one or more additional program outputs for the ATSC DTV channel. As discussed in Chapters 6 and 15, DTV video may be SD or HD, and there may be more than one DTV program output for *multicasting*. Except where indicated, all video equipment described in the following sections is available in either SD or HD versions.

Analog or Digital

The trend in television broadcasting is to replace nearly all analog equipment with digital. This has many advantages, particularly for recording and editing video signals, but also throughout the program chain, and is virtually obligatory for high definition systems. Many local TV stations, however, still have systems for NTSC broadcasting based on composite analog distribution. They then have to convert the analog output to digital to feed the ATSC DTV transmitter. Most network and production centers now work exclusively with digital equipment and distribution systems, and virtually all new studio systems are digital throughout for video, although not always for audio.

Some video equipment is available only in analog form, some only in digital, and other types of equipment are available in both analog and digital versions. As with audio, some digital video equipment, such as a digital server, may be used as a digital "island" in an otherwise analog system, using analog-to-digital and digital-to-analog converters on the unit's input and output.

Compressed or Uncompressed Signal Distribution

As discussed under Bitstream Distribution and Splicing later in this chapter, there are alternative methods for distributing and recording digital signals within the broadcast plant, involving compressed bitstreams in place of baseband signals. This is an area of increasing importance in station design.

File Transfer or Real-Time Video and Audio Distribution

As discussed in both the Video Servers and Ingest and Conversion sections later in this chapter, there is an increasing use of data files for moving program material about. This arrangement uses computer networks instead of standard video and audio distribution, and it fundamentally changes the system design of a television broadcast facility.

Stereo or Surround Sound

Stereo sound has been the norm for NTSC programs and facilities for many years, and this has continued with the use of digital audio facilities for TV. ATSC DTV makes provision for 5.1 channel surround sound, so most production and network centers now have capability for surround sound programming. Many local stations are able to handle 5.1 channels from the network but, at this time, few are equipped to produce their own programs with surround sound.

Much of the audio equipment used in television and radio studios is generally quite similar, so we will concentrate here largely on the video aspects of television. The section on Audio for Television covers the main differences in equipment and systems.

There are, of course, many other considerations for how video and audio systems for television are put together, which are outside the scope of this book.

Studio System

Figure 9.2 is a much-simplified block diagram of a TV production studio system, showing a video switcher with various program sources, including *cameras, video recorders* and *video servers, graphics system, character generator*, and possibly other local and remote sources. It will be apparent that the general arrangement is similar to the radio studio system covered in Chapter 8, but here we are dealing with video sources and signals.

Where a source, such as a video server, provides an audio feed as well as video, then the audio is fed to a separate audio mixer, which

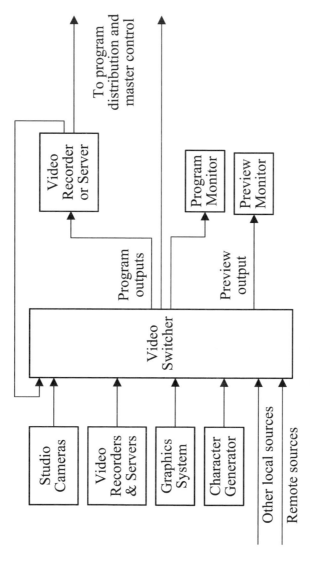

Figure 9.2. Television Production Studio Video Block Diagram

is controlled separately from the video switcher, and which also takes audio-only sources such as the studio microphones, music, and sound effects and produce a program output.

As shown in the figure, there are several outputs from the switcher to feed picture monitors, the video recorder or server, and the program distribution. Not shown on the figure are the picture monitors that are provided for all program sources, or additional outputs for technical monitoring positions such as vision, lighting, and sound operators.

Post-production Edit Suites

Traditional postproduction edit suites also use video switchers for putting together finished programs from prerecorded material, and may be arranged somewhat like a small studio control room. System arrangements are similar to those shown in Figure 9.2, except there are no live cameras and much of the equipment is controlled by an *edit controller*. See the Video Editing section later in this chapter for more information on video editing.

Let's look at the functions of the main components that make up a studio system.

Video Switchers and Effects Units

The heart of the system is the *video switcher*, also known as a *production switcher* and, in Europe, as a *vision mixer*. Figure 9.3 shows an example of the control panel for a fairly sophisticated switcher. The studio sources are fed to switcher inputs, from where they can be switched to feed multiple *buses*, using rows of push buttons as shown in the figure. This process is in fact a video version of the *routing switcher* shown in Figure 8.11 in Chapter 8. One switcher bus feeds direct to the *program* output, and the others feed one or more *mix-effects* (M/E) units. The M/E units enable various *transitions*, including *fade to black*, *cross-fades* or *dissolves*, and *wipes* (where the transition moves across the screen with different, selectable shapes). They also allow *video keying*, where parts of one picture

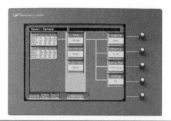

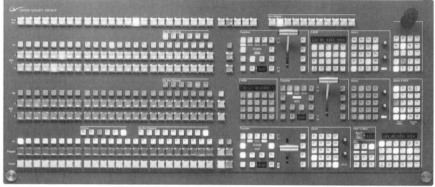

Figure 9.3. Video Switcher Control Panel
Courtesy of Thomson Grass Valley

may be inserted into another, and *chromakeying* (see following section). A *preview* output allows monitoring of any source or effect before it is actually put on air.

Switchers are defined by how many inputs, and how many M/E units, they have. Multiple M/Es allow more than one composite picture to be constructed and transitions to take place from one to the other. Many switchers have a *downstream keyer* (DSK) that allows a final key signal (often a character generator for captions) to be added to the switcher output, downstream of the M/E units. Switchers have basically the same operational features whether they are designed to handle analog or digital, SD or HD, video signals, although the signal processing inside is very different.

Chromakey and Matte Systems

It is often desirable to combine two video signals so that one appears in front of the other. This occurs frequently in weather forecasts, when the presenter appears to be standing in front of, for example, a weather map or satellite picture. This is accomplished using a system called *chromakey*, which is incorporated into most video switchers.

A chromakey system takes one video signal and replaces every part of it that is a user-defined color (typically bright blue or green) with the corresponding video from a second video signal. The result is an output signal, which has combined, selected portions of the two inputs. Let's look at how this works with a weather forecasting set.

On a typical set, the weather forecaster stands in front of a large blank wall or backdrop that is painted one solid color, say blue. The camera is focused on the forecaster, with the wall in the background, and the video from this camera provides the first input signal to the chromakey unit. The second input signal is, say, the satellite video image from a weather graphics system. The chromakey system takes every portion of the image from the camera that matches the blue color of the wall, and replaces it with the corresponding portion of the satellite image. Because the wall should be the only thing that is blue, this replacement creates the illusion in the output picture that the weather forecaster is standing in front of the satellite image. It is important that the forecaster's clothing, hair, skin, and so on should not match the wall, or those elements would also be replaced, and the satellite image would show through.

A chromakey system makes the weather forecaster's job a little tricky because he or she must appear to be pointing to portions of the background picture, but will actually point to places on the blank wall. Typically, somewhere on the set, just out of view of the camera, there is a monitor showing the composite picture of the forecaster and the background image. The forecaster looks at this monitor to ensure that he or she is pointing correctly.

A slightly different system, which does not need a colored background, is known as a *matte system*. In this case, a separate image has to be produced to show which parts of the main image should be replaced. It allows multiple colors in the first video signal to be replaced with video from the second video signal.

Digital Video Effects

Digital video effects (DVE) units enable zooming the picture size for picture-in-picture effects, squeezing it into different shapes, or changing perspective, as well as other effects. DVEs may stand alone or be built into the video switcher, and they may have channels for one or multiple pictures to be processed simultaneously. Some switchers allow sequences of effects with the M/Es and DVEs to be memorized and played back on demand.

DVEs work by storing every pixel of the TV picture in a frame store memory; using powerful computer processing, the pixels are manipulated to change their position in the frame to produce the effect required. Finally, a new frame is reconstructed and read out of the store as a regular video signal. This processing takes place extremely quickly, in *real time*, which means the pictures come out of the DVE as fast as they go in, with only one frame of delay, so the DVE can be used live on air.

Picture and Waveform Monitoring

Picture Monitors

Picture monitors are used to check both program content and technical quality of the video signal. They are used extensively in production studios and throughout all broadcast facilities. The size of a monitor is usually expressed as the picture diagonal measurement, and sizes range from as little as 2 or 3 inches to about 36 inches for a monitor showing a single picture. Monitors may be either 4:3 or 16:9 aspect ratio, depending on the sources being monitored, and these days color monitors are nearly universal. In control rooms, they may be built into a monitor wall, but they are also frequently mounted in control desks or equipment racks in other areas.

Traditionally, cathode ray tube (CRT) displays have been used, for picture monitors, but there is an increasing use of other display technologies, including flat panel plasma and liquid crystal displays (LCD). Plasma and LCDs have advantages of lighter weight and smaller depth than CRTs, but they generally do not produce as high a picture quality, so CRTs have been preferred for critical technical monitoring applications. That situation is now changing as the newer technologies improve.

Very large screens, many feet in width, either using plasma displays or rear-projection units, based on systems such as digital light processing (DLP), are increasingly being used in production and master control rooms. In this case, rather than have many individual monitors for different sources, the large screen is divided up into multiple picture areas, giving the effect of a "virtual monitor wall." One advantage of this arrangement is that the picture sizes and allocations can be easily changed to accommodate different setups, and other information can also be included on the screen, such as source identification, audio level metering, clock, and alarm indicators for fault conditions.

Waveform Monitors

As the name implies, *waveform monitors* are used to measure the technical characteristics of the video waveform (see Chapter 5). In particular, they are used to check the black level and output levels from television cameras, because these parameters have operational controls that are continuously changed during television production. Waveform monitors are also used at different points in the program distribution chain to verify compliance with technical standards.

An analog waveform monitor shows the shape of the actual video signal as it varies in time. However, a digital waveform monitor has to re-create that waveform to its familiar appearance, from the stream of digital video data. Digital waveform monitors are able to perform numerous other checks on the digital video signal.

Traditionally, waveform monitors were stand-alone items of equipment with a dedicated screen. Modern units often have a measurement section at the location where the video signal needs to be monitored and a separate monitor display, which may be at a remote location, with communications over a network. Depending

on the system, the display may also show other information about
the television signal, including the picture itself. Some systems also
allow remote adjustment of the video signal, for correction of black
level, peak level, and other parameters.

Vectorscope

A *vectorscope* is a special sort of waveform monitor that shows only
the video chrominance information in a *polar display* (parameters are
shown as vectors, with a distance and angle from the center of the
screen). Its primary use is with analog composite video, where it is
important to check that the color subcarrier is correctly adjusted.
Signals for each color appears at a different location on the screen,
so the six primary and secondary colors of standard color bars have
boxes marked on the screen for where they should be.

Television Cameras

Studio Cameras

Studio cameras are designed to produce high picture quality and
have many features for convenience and ease of use, including
large *viewfinders*, the ability to have high-quality large lenses with
wide zoom ranges, and comprehensive monitoring and communications. When necessary, they can be fitted with *teleprompters*,
which are special electronic displays of script for presenters to read,
while looking into the camera lens. It is not easy to provide all of
these features on small, lightweight cameras, so studio cameras
tend to be fairly substantial, as shown in Figure 9.4.

Studio cameras are connected through a *camera cable* to a *camera
control unit* (CCU) in the equipment area associated with the studio
control room. This unit provides power and communication links
to the camera (so the operator can hear and talk to the staff in the
control room using a headset). It enables the camera output to be
fed to the video switcher and allows for remote controls in
the vision control room to adjust and match the appearance of
the camera picture.

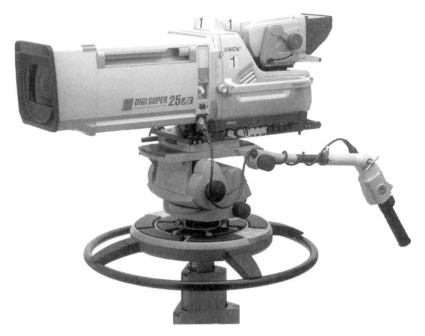

Figure 9.4. Television Studio Camera
Courtesy of Sony

Portable Cameras

Small, portable cameras at one time sacrificed performance for portability and were used primarily for news gathering, where light weight and low power consumption were more important than picture quality. However, current generation portable cameras are now available for both SD and HD with similar performance to the best studio cameras. They are, therefore, being used in all aspects of television production inside and outside the studio. Most portable cameras have built-in (or can be fitted with) a video recorder of some sort (i.e., they are a camcorder) and are powered from a battery, so they are portable and self-contained. This arrangement is universal for news gathering and most field production (see Chapter 10).

When used in a studio, portable cameras are fitted with an adaptor allowing use with a camera cable and CCU, as with a studio camera. They may be handheld, or used with camera support devices, and they may also be fitted with special mounts for large lenses and large viewfinders, thus providing many of the capabilities of studio cameras.

Lenses

Most imaging starts with light passing through a lens. Television cameras use *zoom lenses* that have adjustable focal lengths. At the *telephoto* end of the zoom range, the camera sees a small amount of the scene, which is enlarged to fill the frame. At the *wide-angle* end of the range, it sees much more of the scene, as though from farther away.

The camera operator adjusts the lens zoom and focus settings with controls mounted on the *pan bars* at the back of the camera, while looking at the camera picture in the viewfinder. There may be a *shot-box* that allows the operator to preset different lens settings and go instantly to them at the push of a button. The *aperture* of the lens is adjusted by the vision engineer in the control room.

Camera Imaging

The scanning process for video images was explained in Chapter 5. To recap, when a TV camera is pointed at a scene, the image passes through the lens and is focused onto a light-sensitive pickup device of some sort. The target or sensor produces variations in the electric charge-density level; it is scanned to dissect the picture into scan lines, and this process is repeated to produce sequential fields and frames. Based on the amount of light detected at any point in time, the camera produces a voltage that is proportional to the amount of light at each point in the picture.

Note that each frame in the camera is scanned bottom to top, whereas in a picture display device it is top to bottom. This is because the image produced by the camera lens is actually upside down, so the scan also has to be inverted.

The device that did the image scanning in older television cameras was a *camera tube*, or *pickup tube*. An electron beam actually scanned the electric charge on the inside surface of the tube to create the electronic version of the video image. In most modern cameras, the image pickup device is called a *charge coupled device*, or CCD.

CCDs for cameras use a pair of electronic matrices (a two-dimensional array), as shown in principle in Figure 9.5. Each matrix comprises a very large number of individual photosensitive "cells." The number of cells determines the resolution of the camera, and many more cells are needed for an HD camera compared to SD. Each cell in the first matrix is charged up to a level that is proportional to the amount of light falling on it. The individual charges from each of the cells in the first matrix are transferred simultaneously 30 times per second to corresponding cells in a second matrix, which is shielded from the light. The circuitry in the camera then scans the second matrix, and the samples from each cell are processed to produce the video signal.

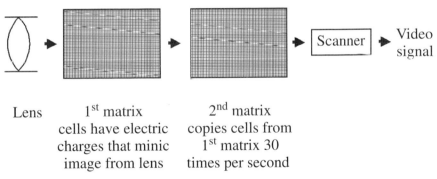

Lens   1st matrix   2nd matrix
       cells have electric   copies cells from
       charges that minic   1st matrix 30
       image from lens   times per second

Figure 9.5. CCD Imaging Process

The charges in the first matrix must be transferred to a second matrix before they are scanned because the first matrix charge levels are constantly changing as the image through the lens changes. So, a "snapshot" of the first matrix must be created to ensure that the correct fixed image is converted to an electrical signal by the camera. Depending on the camera, the CCDs may be scanned to produce an output image with 4:3 or 16:9 aspect ratio, or in some designs it is switchable to either format.

The best-performing CCD color cameras, as used for broadcasting, actually use three CCDs—one each to scan the electric charge image created by the red, green, and blue light coming through the lens. As shown in Figure 9.6, the light from the lens passes through an optical *beam splitter*, based on glass prisms, which splits the incoming optical image into three different color beams (red, green, and blue). The beams then pass through additional filters, which remove any remaining unwanted colors, and the purified individual color images fall onto their own individual CCDs, where they are scanned, as described previously.

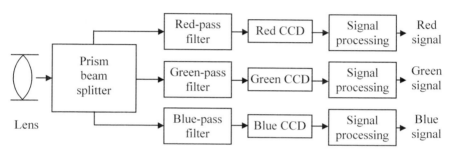

Figure 9.6. Basic Design of a Three-CCD Camera

A new generation of pickup devices based on Complementary Metal Oxide Semiconductor (CMOS) technology has been introduced. This enables cameras that are smaller in size and with low power consumption. Development is ongoing, and it is likely that both CCD and CMOS devices will be used in television cameras for some time to come.

The three separate color signals that come from the three pickup devices are *component video* signals. These are further processed and may be fed out of the camera as three separate analog component signals. However, most cameras carry out analog-to-digital conversion and produce a serial digital video output (SD or HD, depending on the camera type), as described in Chapter 6. An SD camera may combine the analog component signals to produce an NTSC composite video signal, as described in Chapter 5.

HD cameras often provide a *downconverted* digital SD or composite analog video output as well as the HD feed. This provides extra flexibility in how the camera signals may be used.

Camera Support

Portable cameras may be handheld (most actually rest on the cameraperson's shoulder), but, whenever possible, cameras are fixed to some sort of mount. This is less tiring for the operator and allows for pictures without *camera shake*. Both portable and studio camera types may be mounted on a *pan-and-tilt head*, which allows the camera to be smoothly pointed in the right direction. In studios, this head is mounted on a wheeled *pedestal*, which adjusts smoothly up and down, or on a tripod with a wheeled *skid*, both of which allow the camera to be *tracked* across the floor. For special high- or low-angle shots, cameras may be mounted on an elevating *crane* or a counterbalanced *boom*.

Some news studios do not use a camera operator, so the camera is mounted on a *robotic pedestal* with remote controls in the control room for camera positioning and lens zoom and focus.

Isocam

In a live production environment, the various cameras are selected and switched through the video switcher, to produce the final output. This output can be recorded for subsequent editing and replay. An alternative arrangement is often used where multicamera shows are recorded for subsequent editing. In that case, the output of all cameras is recorded simultaneously, so they are all available during the postproduction process. This arrangement is known as *isocam* (presumably from "isolated camera").

Film in Television

Acquisition

The aforementioned process describes the use of electronic cameras to acquire video images. However, many television programs are actually shot with film cameras, both in studios and outside on location, using techniques similar to those used for making cinema films. Some directors prefer working with film, and some television executives just prefer the "look" of film-produced pictures.

Most productions shot on film use 35 millimeter film cameras for the highest quality. Low-budget productions, and especially those shot in remote locations with portable cameras, may use 16 millimeter film, with smaller and lighter cameras and lower film costs. Traditionally, film was edited by cutting and splicing the negative, with special effects produced in optical printers. The finished film was then played out or transferred to videotape using a *telecine* machine.

These days, however, most film material is transferred to video soon after processing. From postproduction onward, the process is then the same as for video-produced material. Thirty-five-millimeter film can produce excellent pictures for both SD and HD video, while 16 millimeter film is usually more suited to SD, because its resolution limitations, marginal image stability, and film grain can result in image quality that is inferior to electronic HD pictures.

Telecines

A *telecine* scans film frames and produces a regular video signal output. One type of telecine, used for many years, was basically a film projector mated to a device like a television camera. Instead of the optical image from the projector falling on a screen, it was directed into the camera lens and each frame was scanned while the film was stationary in the *film gate*. Some types of modern telecines split the light from the film into red, green, and blue beams and use three *area-array CCD pickup devices* to scan each frame. Other telecines use three *line-array CCD* devices to detect the light shone through the film frame, after it has been split into red, green, and blue components. With this system, the film moves continuously past the scanner, and the motion of the film produces the effect of vertical scanning as described for NTSC video in Chapter 5, while the horizontal scan is performed by the row of CCD cells. An older system, which is still used in some facilities, is the *flying spot scanner*. In this design, the light shining through the film comes from a moving spot of light emitted by a high-intensity cathode ray tube (CRT). This "flying" spot scans the film as it moves continuously past the scanner. The motion of the spot and the motion of the film together produce the effect of horizontal and vertical scanning. The light is split into red, green, and blue beams and detected by three *photomultiplier* devices. In both CCD and flying spot telecines, considerable signal processing is required to produce the final video output signal, usually including an electronic frame store. Most telecine transfers also include the process of *color correction*, to correct color casts and other anomalies of the pictures on film.

At one time, telecines were widely used by networks and broadcast stations for broadcasting feature films and news shot on film. Most stations no longer use such machines, and they are used mainly by post-houses for transferring film to video.

Film Scanners

The best-quality high definition film transfers are done with a *film scanner*, rather than a telecine. This device uses CCDs with very high resolution and produces a digital data file output rather than a video signal. The transfers may take place in slower than real time, thus allowing very high quality to be achieved. The output file is then available for postproduction work.

3:2 Pulldown

Film runs at 24 frames per second, while U.S. television video uses approximately 30 frames per second. A system called *3:2 pulldown* is used so that film images can be transferred to video. You will remember from Chapter 5 that NTSC uses two fields for each frame so there are 60 fields per second. In the 3:2 system, the first film frame of any consecutive pair is converted by the telecine into three video fields, while the second film frame is converted into two video fields, and so on consecutively. The two film frames occupy 2/24 of a second, which is 1/12 of a second, and the five (3 + 2) video fields occupy 5/60 of a second, which is also 1/12 of a second; so the timing works out exactly over any five-field period.

One result of the 3:2 pulldown sequence is that moving objects in the picture exhibit a slight but noticeable judder, because alternate film frames are each effectively displayed for different lengths of time. Some modern DTV receivers can perform a process called *reverse 3:2 pulldown* that effectively reverses the process and allows for smoother motion to be portrayed, with a progressive scan image.

Videotape Recorders

Videotape recorders (VTRs) are rapidly being replaced by hard disk–based servers in many studio applications and by optical disk and solid-state flash memory recorders for portable use. There is, however, a huge installed base of different types of VTRs still in existence, and this form of storage has formed the backbone of television operations for many years, and will not disappear completely for some time. We therefore cover the topic in some detail.

VTRs have some similarities to their audio counterparts, and they all use magnetic tape as the media on which the program material is stored. Early VTRs used tape stored on open reels, but all modern machines house the tape in a cassette for protection.

As well as recording video signals, VTRs record two or more channels of audio information and a *timecode* signal (see later section on SMPTE timecode). A control track is also usually recorded on tape for machine synchronization during playback. Arrangements vary somewhat, depending on the particular format and, in particular, whether the VTR uses analog or digital recording.

Different types of VTR are defined by the video format it can handle and the *tape format*. This includes not only the physical characteristics of the tape but also all aspects of the way the signals are recorded. If a recording is made on one machine with a particular format, it should play back on any other machine of the same format. Many different tape formats were developed at different times and by different manufacturers, each with their own characteristics as summarized in the sections for analog and digital VTRs.

Magnetic Recording

It is beyond the scope of this book to explain exactly how video recording works, so we will just mention a few of the basic principles. As with audio, video signals are recorded onto tape with a *record head* that converts the electrical signal voltage into a varying magnetic field. This magnetizes the tape coating as the tape moves past the head. Upon playback, the head picks up the stored magnetic information and converts it back into an electrical signal voltage.

The higher the frequencies that have to be recorded, the higher the speed at which the tape must pass the record and playback head. Because video signals have much higher frequencies than audio, a much higher tape speed is needed. Digital video signals contain higher frequencies still, and need even higher speeds. However, it is not practical to pull the tape past a stationary head at a high enough speed, so the problem is overcome using a system called *helical scan*, also known as *slant track* recording.

Helical Scan

With the exception of the obsolete quadraplex VTR, all practical VTRs rely on *helical scan* to achieve the high head-to-tape speed needed for video recording. Details vary, but the principle is the same for all machines, as shown in Figure 9.7.

Two or more record and playback heads are fixed to the outside of a rapidly rotating drum, around which the tape is wrapped at an angle, like part of a spiral helix (hence, the name). The tape moves quite slowly past the drum, but each head moves rapidly across the surface of the tape, laying down a series of diagonal tracks. The angles shown in the figure are exaggerated, so the tracks are much longer than shown in the figure.

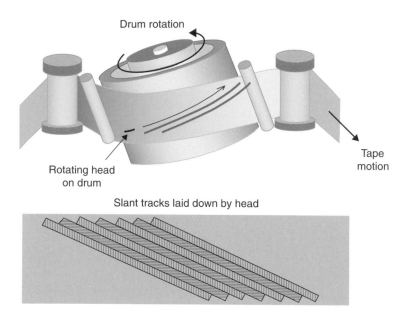

Figure 9.7. Principle of Helical Scan Recording

Because it is not practical to record video signals directly onto tape, various modulated carriers are used for different VTR formats, digital and analog being quite different. The video information on the slant tracks, recorded by the *rotating heads*, takes up most of the tape area. There may also be fixed heads that record and playback audio, control, and timecode signals on narrow *longitudinal tracks* along each edge of the tape (not shown in the figure). These tracks vary with different machines and, in some cases, the audio and/or timecode signals may also be recorded on the slant tracks using the rotating heads. In the case of digital VTRs, the audio is embedded with the video bitstream and recorded to tape with the rotating heads.

Timebase Correctors

Videotape recording for broadcasting would not have become possible without the invention of the *timebase corrector* (TBC). Because a VTR is a mechanical device, there are slight variations in the speed of the tape and the rotation of the drum. These produce irregularities in the timing of the replayed video signal, and the sync pulses and picture information may arrive at slightly the wrong time. The timing variations are not important if the signal has only to feed a television set direct (as a consumer VCR does). In that case, the set will remain locked to the sync pulses even as they vary and will produce a basically stable picture. Such time-base errors are disastrous in a broadcast station, however, where the signal has to be mixed with other signals, perhaps edited, and re-recorded. To make VTR output signals usable, they are passed through a TBC that comprises an electronic buffer store. This removes the input irregularities and sends out video with stable timing restored.

Digital TBCs offer a much greater correction range than analog and are universally used, even with VTRs that otherwise record an analog signal on tape. However, VTRs that record a digital signal on tape do not actually have a separate TBC function, because the techniques required to recover the digital data from the tape also take care of correcting any timing irregularities.

In approximate historical order of introduction, we list below the principal videotape formats you may come across, with their main characteristics. Some of the machines mentioned are now obsolete and may be found only in specialist facilities for dubbing archive material onto more modern formats, but they are included for completeness. There are other less well-known formats, which are not listed. With the exception of Quadraplex and Type C, all VTRs described use tape on two reels and enclosed in a cassette for protection, so this is not mentioned each time.

Slow and Fast Motion

Most VTRs are able to produce pictures at speeds both slower and faster than when they were recorded, by speeding up and slowing down the tape. There is a limited range of speeds over which the pictures retain broadcast quality, depending on the format.

Analog VTRs

Two-Inch Quadraplex (1956)

Developed by Ampex Corporation in the United States, and also known as *Quad*, this format is now completely obsolete and is mentioned here only because it was the first successful VTR format. The name comes from the wheel with four heads, which rotated across the width of the tape to produce the video tracks. The system used open reels of two-inch-wide tape, which were extremely heavy and cumbersome, but at one time were the means by which nearly all television program material was shipped from one place to another.

U-Matic (1970)

The U-Matic format, developed by a Japanese consortium, used 3/4 inch tape. Video quality was not particularly high, but it improved considerably with the later High Band version. The format is still in regular use by some stations and production houses and machines are still manufactured on a limited basis. Portable versions were once widely used for news gathering, as a replacement for 16 millimeter film.

Type C (1976)

The Type C format, developed by Ampex in the United States and Sony in Japan, used one-inch tape on open reels to record composite video, with two channels of audio. It was the first machine to provide usable still frame, slow- and fast-motion playback, and pictures in shuttle. At one time, this was the most widely used VTR format, but it has now largely disappeared from regular use.

VHS (1976) and S-VHS (1987)

Developed by JVC, VHS (Video Home System) is the very successful standard format for consumer VCRs, using a 1/2 inch tape. It is used in homes and businesses throughout the world.

The S-VHS version has higher resolution, delivers better color performance, and can record timecode. It is also very cost effective, so it has been used by some small-market broadcasters, but it has largely been superseded by other, higher-quality professional formats.

Betacam (1982) and BetacamSP (1986)

The Betacam format, from Sony, uses 1/2 inch videotape to record analog video. Input and output interfaces use composite video, but the signal is actually recorded on tape in analog component form. This considerably improves picture quality. BetacamSP (superior performance), with different tape and higher recording frequencies, further improves the quality. BetacamSP became the industry workhorse for portable recording and studio applications before digital formats were introduced, many of these recorders are still in use today and new BetacamSP machines are still being manufactured.

Video8 (1983) and Hi8 (1989)

These formats, using 8 millimeter tape, were developed by Sony for consumer camcorders, in conjunction with several other manufacturers. Hi8 was occasionally used for professional assignments requiring a very small camcorder, before the introduction of digital MiniDV.

M (1983) and M-II (1985)

These formats from Panasonic, using 1/2 inch tape, were developed for professional use from the VHS format. They were direct competitors to Betacam and BetacamSP but were not widely adopted and are now obsolete.

Digital VTRs

There are many legacy analog VTRs still in use but digital VTRs have largely replaced analog machines for new systems due to there superior video and audio performance and other advantages.

One crucial advantage of digital VTRs is the ability to record many *generations* of video without degradation. This is important with editing and postproduction, where the original material needs to be re-recorded many times. Analog recordings show a buildup of video noise and other degradations after a very few generations, which does not occur with digital.

Figure 9.8 shows an example of a standard definition Digital Betacam VTR.

Figure 9.8. Studio Digital VTR
Courtesy of Sony

Video Compression for Recording

It is possible to record video signals onto tape in uncompressed form. However, uncompressed video has a high data rate (270 or 360 Mbps for SD, 1.485 Gbps for HD), so many digital VTRs reduce the amount of data by using *video compression*, while trying to maintain quality as high as possible. This allows smaller tape sizes and smaller head drums to be used, which can make the machine more compact, and also allows less tape to be consumed. MPEG compression, as used for ATSC transmission (see Chapter 15), is used for some VTRs, but with lower compression ratios than used for transmission. Several other compression systems are also used for recording.

The digital VTRs listed first are all designed to record standard definition video only.

D1 (1987)

The first digital VTR was developed by Sony to record the new 601 component video format defined by the CCIR (later known as ITU-R BT.601—see Chapter 6 on digital video). It used 19 millimeter tape, with a recording time up to 76 minutes of uncompressed video. The machine was expensive and used mainly for post-production, where its multiple generation capability was important. It is no longer widely used.

D2 (1989)

Produced by both Sony and Ampex, the D2 format was unusual in that it recorded composite NTSC (or PAL) video in digital form. It used 19 millimeter tape, with up to three hours of record time. While allowing easy integration into existing analog facilities, it was eventually overtaken by component video recorders for new installations.

D3 (1991)

The D3 format came from Panasonic and also recorded composite video in digital form. It used 1/2 inch tape, with up to four hours of record time. With an alternative small cassette, it was possible to make equipment suitable for electronic news gathering (ENG) and other portable applications.

Digital Betacam (1993)

Developed by Sony, with some decks also able to play back analog BetacamSP tapes, this format uses light 2:1 compression recording component video. Quality is excellent, and the machine has become the industry standard for high-quality standard definition recording for portable and studio applications.

D5 (1994)

D5 was produced by Panasonic as a development of D3 and records component video with four audio channels onto 1/2 inch tape. It uses a higher data rate than Digital Betacam and records uncompressed video at up to 360 Mbps for the very highest quality, but it has the disadvantage of not being available in a portable recorder version.

DV and MiniDV (1995)

Developed by a consortium of ten companies, this format was intended for consumer camcorders. It records video and two audio channels onto 1/4 inch tape, with 5:1 compression using the DV codec. Maximum recording time in standard mode is 80 minutes. This format is now also widely used for professional products.

DVCPRO (1995) and DVCPRO50 (1998)

DVCPRO from Panasonic was a development of the DV format for broadcast applications, using a wider track and a different tape material to increase robustness and quality. It also records longitudinal cue and control tracks for improved editing performance. This format is widely used by broadcasters, particularly for ENG, and has a good range of portable and studio recorders and editing facilities. The later DVCPRO50 further improves quality by recording at a higher bit rate (50 Mbps), at the expense of reduced recording time.

D9 Digital-S (1995)

This format, developed by JVC, uses a 1/2 inch tape cassette, similar to VHS, but is, in fact, a much higher-quality professional machine, rivaling Digital Betacam. It uses a variant of the DV codec, with some similarities to that used for DVCPRO50, but with a different tape format, and is available in both portable and studio versions.

DVCAM (1996)

This is the Sony professional version of DV, with quality and capabilities similar to DVCPRO.

Betacam SX (1996)

This format from Sony was targeted for ENG and newsroom applications, using quite heavy 10:1 video compression. Betacam SX VTRs were the first to allow video to be sent back to the studio over video links at twice the normal speed.

Digital8 (1999)

This format from Sony records the same digital signal as DV onto less expensive Hi8 tapes, and can play back analog Video8 and Hi8 tapes. Intended as a consumer camcorder format, there is now also an ultra-compact editing deck and the format is occasionally used for very low cost professional applications.

IMX (2000)

This Sony format has some similarities to Digital Betacam but uses MPEG compression and is able to record eight audio channels. As well as regular playback of video and audio, the recorded compressed data can be output directly from the tape, for transferring to video servers.

HD Digital VTRs

These VTRs are all intended for recording high definition video signals with either 1080 or 720 lines of resolution.

D5 HD (1994)

This HD format from Panasonic is based on the SD D5 recorder and uses 4:1 Motion JPEG video compression to record video and four audio channels (eight channels on later models). It provides high-quality HD recordings and is widely used as a mastering machine, but is available only as a studio recorder.

HDCAM (1997)

This Sony HD format is based on the Digital Betacam recorder mechanics. Compared to D5, this format has more aggressive compression, of about 7:1 and, in order to reduce the data rate sufficiently for the tape format, it subsamples the video to a horizontal resolution of 1440 pixels for the 1080-line format, compared to 1920 for D5 HD. It is available in both studio and portable versions and is widely used for high definition program acquisition.

DVCPRO HD (2000)

This HD version of the DVCPRO format from Panasonic records video with considerably higher compression and more aggressive subsampling than used for either D5 or HDCAM, to achieve a bit rate of 100 Mbps recorded on tape. It also subsamples the video to a horizontal resolution of only 1280 pixels for the 1080-line format.

D9 HD (2000)

This HD version of Digital-S from JVC records video and up to 8 channels of audio at a data rate of 100 Mbps, using a codec developed by JVC.

HDCAM SR (2004)

This new version of HDCAM, from Sony, records HD video at a data rate of 440 Mbps with full 1920 × 1080 resolution, using mild compression of only 2.5:1, and with up to two hours of recording time. It carries 12 channels of uncompressed audio and is intended for the highest-quality production and distribution applications.

HDV (2004)

Sony, JVC, Canon, and Sharp have agreed to an HDV standard for consumer and professional use. HDV records an HD signal to MiniDV tapes using heavy MPEG-2 compression and aggressive subsampling to permit recording at 25 Mbps, with a recording time of 60 minutes. The format is based on technology previously developed by JVC. Both camcorders and studio recorders have been announced.

Optical, Solid-State, and Hard Disk Recorders

XDCAM (2003)

The XDCAM recording format from Sony uses an optical disk for recording SD digital video and audio. The disc is similar to, but not the same as, Blu-ray DVD and can be recorded, erased, and re-recorded. SD signals are recorded with a choice of compression formats, including DVCAM and IMX, with up to 85 minutes of program. Files can be accessed and transferred direct from the disc to other systems such as video servers. XDCAM is available as a camcorder and studio recorder and is intended to be part of an integrated system for managing digital video content.

P2 (2003)

The P2 recording format from Panasonic uses solid-state memory for recording either SD or HD digital video and audio and has the advantage of containing no moving parts. The recorder uses up to five Secure Digital flash memory plug-in cards, each currently of up to 4 GB capacity. Signals are recorded with DV or DVCPRO compression, giving up to 18 minutes of video per card with standard definition. P2 is available as a camcorder and studio recorder. Both support MXF file transfer (see later section) and are intended to be part of an integrated system for managing digital content.

Hard Disk

Ikegami, Sony, and JVC have all produced portable camera systems with dockable modules that record digital video and audio direct to a hard disk. The recorded files can be transferred at high speed from the hard disk direct to a video server or nonlinear editing system (see later sections).

Video Editing

In the early days of quadraplex VTRs, videotape was edited by actually cutting and splicing the tape. This crude system soon gave way to editing by copying (*dubbing*) portions of the source VTR material onto a second VTR. This method provides *cuts-only* edits, without any other transitions. Current VTR editing suites typically have several playback VTRs for the program material sources (known as *A-roll, B-roll*, and so on), fed through a video switcher to allow transitions with mixes, wipes, and effects to be carried out. Graphics, captions, and other elements may also be added at the same time. The output of the switcher with the finished program is fed to a record VTR.

All of the machines and the switcher are controlled by an *edit controller*. This system locates the right program material and tells the VTRs when to start and stop and when to record. The controller monitors the tape *timecode* to know exactly which piece of program material is playing at any particular time.

The edit controller uses an *edit decision list* (EDL), which has all of the instructions for assembling the program. This includes which tape reels are needed and the particular timecode readings for the beginning and end of each segment to be included in the program. EDLs may be prepared in the edit suite, but they are frequently prepared *off-line*, using copies of the program material recorded on a low-cost tape format such as VHS or MiniDV, with *burnt-in timecode*.

Such facilities, however, are frequently being replaced by nonlinear editing systems, where many of the effects previously done with a video switcher can be achieved more efficiently using the editing system software. It is also possible, however, to use some edit control systems with both VTRs and *video servers*, enabling integrated postproduction with both types of recording system.

SMPTE Timecode

For video production, editing, and transmission, it is necessary to time program segments accurately and also to be able to identify any single frame of video. For this purpose, the Society of Motion Picture and Television Engineers (SMPTE) developed a system called *SMPTE Time and Control Code*, usually known as *timecode*. This digital code is recorded onto videotape to identify how many hours, minutes, seconds, and video frames have passed since the beginning of the recording. On early analog VTRs, timecode was recorded on a separate track along the edge of the tape—this is known as *longitudinal (or linear) timecode* (LTC). The disadvantages of LTC are that it takes up extra space on the tape and cannot be read when the tape is stationary or moving slowly. A later development puts timecode in the vertical interval of the video signal (see Chapter 5), where it is known as *vertical interval timecode* (VITC). VITC can be read at most tape speeds (whenever the video is locked), which is a great advantage during editing or when cueing a tape for broadcast. For maximum flexibility, some VTRs and editing systems can use both LTC and VITC.

SMPTE timecode is recorded when the video is first recorded; it can then be used to identify edit points during postproduction. If necessary, a new continuous timecode is laid down for a finished program. This can then be used for timing and machine control purposes, in conjunction with an automation system, when the tape is played out for broadcast.

Timecode is now used with video servers and nonlinear editing systems. It has many other applications: it can, for example, be used to synchronize a separately recorded audio recording with a video recording, control station clocks, and act as the time reference for station automation.

Burnt-in timecode is used where an editor, producer, or other viewer needs to view program material and also see the timecode at the same time, to determine edit points. The timecode numbers are keyed into the video, so they will always be visible, allowing a copy to be made onto a low-cost tape format such as VHS or MiniDV, which can be viewed *off-line*, away from the editing suite facility.

Video Servers

We discussed in Chapter 8 how hard disk recorders for audio have revolutionized radio broadcasting. The equivalent development in television is the *video server*, which is widely used for recording, editing, storing, and distributing digital video signals. A video server is basically a powerful computer that is capable of receiving digital video signals, storing them on hard drives, and playing them back when required. As with audio servers, video servers can playback material while still recording, and stored material can be played back at random by multiple users.

Recording Formats and Interfaces

Although called video servers, these devices in fact record both audio and video. They accept signals over standard video and audio interfaces but, like all computer data, the video and audio is stored on the hard disk system in the form of files. The video may be stored uncompressed (sometimes known as *linear* recording) or, to reduce the size of the files, it may be stored in compressed form (particularly for HD format signals, which produce very large files). Several systems are used for video compression, largely based on the same methods as used with digital videotape recorders.

When a digital video file is retrieved from a server system and sent, say, to a video switcher, the playback device reads the file from the disk, formats it into an SMPTE 259M (SD) or SMPTE 292M (HD) serial data stream, and sends it out to the switcher. Similarly, the server retrieves the audio data and sends it out as an AES/EBU digital audio stream. Servers also have a network interface for receiving and distributing files over a LAN or WAN.

Server Types

There are many varieties of video servers. Some are based on standard computers, with the usual keyboard, mouse, and monitor for the operator interface. However, most broadcast servers use custom hardware optimized for video applications and with provision for all of the video and audio input and output interfaces. Some versions provide front-panel controls with buttons, knobs, and indicators for specific functions, similar to a videotape recorder.

Video servers may be associated with a production studio, a post-production facility, an on-air news studio, or a master control switcher for transmission. In most cases, they are connected to a computer network and, hence, able to share files. A large video server system, therefore, can provide the functions of both a library and a distribution system. An example of a server-based playout system is shown in Figure 9.9 later in this chapter.

Archiving

Although server systems can record large amounts of programming on hard drives, when a station puts all of its program library onto the system, it may run out of hard drive capacity. To efficiently store programming for archive purposes, the material may be transferred to special magnetic data tapes, which can store very large amounts of data for long periods with great reliability. The disadvantage of this storage method is slow access to any particular program item.

File Interchange and MXF

The file formats used by different servers are often different, depending on the manufacturers of the particular system. This can make interchange of program files among producers, networks, and stations rather difficult. A new standard developed by SMPTE, known as MXF (for *Material eXchange Format*), makes such interchange much easier. MXF enables systems from different vendors to "talk" to each other for exchange of video and audio material and to include all the *metadata* (information about the program material) that is needed to make optimum use of the program material.

Slow and Fast Motion

Servers are well suited to producing video with either slow or fast motion as recorded frames can be easily processed without concern for retrieval from tape at nonstandard speeds. Systems are available that are specially designed for playing back slow and fast motion. The quality of slow-motion images is also improved considerably by using a camera that produces images with higher than normal frame rates.

Nonlinear Editing

As with digital audio, which can be edited on a PC or dedicated audio workstation, video nonlinear editing may be carried out on a high-power general-purpose PC fitted with an editing software program, suitable input and output interface cards, and sufficient hard disk storage. Alternatively, some sophisticated editing systems use dedicated custom hardware, although at their core, they all incorporate computer processors and hard disk storage. In all systems, program material can be selected, cut, reordered, modified, and generally prepared for transmission.

One big advantage of disk-based systems, compared to traditional tape-based editing, is the ability to instantly access any program segment and also to go back and revise edits made earlier in the program, without affecting later edits. This *random access* feature allows *nonlinear editing*, which is in sharp contrast to having to shuttle a tape backward and forward to locate a particular program segment.

All nonlinear editors provide at least some of the functions of both a video switcher and audio mixing console, but implemented in software. This allows pictures and sound to be modified, and several sources to be mixed and combined together, often with special effects, all carried out on the computer. In fact, many functions for television postproduction, which previously needed a room full of equipment, can be done on a PC with a few add-on items of equipment. This has allowed new ways of programming and has blurred the definition of what is really needed for TV production and postproduction.

Digitizing

Depending on how the program material is originally recorded, it may be necessary to transfer it to the editing system in a process known as *digitizing*. The video is played back and passed through a processor, which records it to the system's hard drive in a suitable compressed or uncompressed format. One advantage of systems such as the P2 solid-state recorder (see earlier section) is that the field camcorder records the signals in files on the P2 card, which can be instantly used in an editing system, without further digitizing being needed.

File Interchange and AAF

As with video servers, the file formats used by different nonlinear editing systems are often different, depending on the manufacturers of the particular system. This has complicated the interchange of program material during the program production and postproduction process. A recently developed standard known as AAF (for Advance Authoring Format) makes such interchange much easier. AAF is compatible with MXF and makes provision for the specific types of metadata that accompanies program material during the production and postproduction process.

Character Generators and Computer Graphics

Character Generators

A *character generator* is basically a computer system for producing captions, text, and simple graphics for adding to a video program. It may be a regular PC equipped to output video signals and running special software or it may be a dedicated, integrated hardware/software system.

Text input may come from a keyboard or from a communications port. The user can select the background color and the font, format, and color for the text, and how it is displayed on screen (e.g., as rolling titles). In addition to alphanumeric characters, character generators also allow other digital images, such as logos, to be recalled from storage and added to the screen.

All titles and other pages of text that are generated can be saved and stored on a hard drive. They can then be recalled and replayed on demand when needed in a program.

An example of how keyboard input to a character generator might be used would be when a news reporter's name is added to the bottom of the screen during a newscast. An example of an external source supplying data to a character generator through the data port would be when a warning about a weather emergency is received by a television station's Emergency Alert System equipment, and the warning is automatically fed out over the air, using the character generator to scroll a text message across the screen.

Graphics and Paint Systems

Graphics systems may be based on PC platforms, or high-end systems may use dedicated, integrated hardware and software. They provide the capability for producing all types of graphic art, charts, pictures, animations, and so on and may be interfaced to other systems for importing data and other images, such as financial information or weather maps.

Paint systems simulate regular artist painting methods and provide a special user interface to allow full artistic expression. This includes a *graphics tablet* on which the operator "paints" with a pressure-sensitive electronic "brush," producing images on the screen.

Electronic Newsroom

The news production process involves editing of program material from tapes provided by news gathering crews or recorded from remote sources through the ingest system. Stock footage has to be located and made available for editing, and suitable graphics need to be produced to add to the story. At the same time, the scripts for the news stories are prepared separately and brought together with the audio and video program material at the time of transmission.

An *electronic newsroom* brings all of these functions together in one system, using video server–based recording, nonlinear editing, graphics systems, databases, special software, and multiple work-stations running special software, all connected by a network. This allows most of the news preparation functions to be integrated, so the people involved can work cooperatively to produce the news stories from their own desktops, while accessing the same material from central servers.

Such systems often provide low-resolution *proxy* video to users on their PCs, for use while preparing the news story. This reduces the load on the network and servers that would occur if everyone had access to the full-resolution version.

For transmission, the electronic newsroom system provides the story scripts for the presenter to read and plays out the high-quality version of the finished news stories at the right times.

Signal Distribution

Signal distribution is one of the less glamorous aspects of television engineering—there are no flashy control panels, cameras, recorders, or even pictures to see. Nevertheless, it is one of the most important aspects of station design. The design choices made are fundamental to the way the station works and may be difficult to change at a later date. All of the System Considerations discussed earlier in this chapter affect the equipment used for signal distribution. Audio system and distribution issues were discussed in Chapter 8, and they largely apply also to television systems. Many components make up the overall system, but the main ones include the following.

System Interconnections

The way video signals are transported between different items of equipment, and between different areas in a television facility, is similar whether the signals are analog or digital, SD or HD. Video interconnections within the facility use *coaxial cable* (also known as *coax*). The main difference for digital is that digital video signals, especially HD, with data rates up to 1.485 Gbps, require coax with very good high-frequency response to carry the signals without degradation. Even then, HD cable runs are limited to about 1000 feet. SD video, both analog and digital, may run considerably longer than this. For very long runs, up to many miles, video signals may be carried over *fiber-optic* cables.

Compressed bitstreams (see Bitstream Distribution and Splicing, later in this chapter) are also transported within the station on coaxial cable, in much the same way as serial digital video.

Interchange of files between video servers and other equipment uses computer network technologies, with switches, routers, and LAN cabling as discussed in Chapter 7.

Video Patch Panel

Video patch panels serve a similar purpose to the audio patch panels, described in Chapter 8, for testing and cross-connecting program signals. They use a different type of jack, designed for video, with those intended for HD digital video requiring a much better frequency response specification than those for analog signals.

Video Routing Switcher

Most stations have a *video routing switcher* (also known as a *router* or *matrix*) to distribute signals to multiple locations in the facility. Functions are similar to the audio routing switcher described in Chapter 8, but for video, and different versions are needed for analog, SD digital, and HD digital. In many cases, video and audio routing switchers are linked together as separate *levels* of a single unit, to switch both video and audio signals together.

Video Distribution Amplifier

A *video distribution amplifier* (referred to as a DA) has the same function for video as the audio DA described in Chapter 8, for distributing signals to multiple destinations. Video DAs come in analog and digital versions, for both SD and HD. They may also incorporate *cable equalizers* that adjust the frequency response of the amplifier to compensate for the high frequency loss of the cable connected to the amplifier. This is important to maintain video quality when feeding signals over long lengths of cable.

Embedded Audio

To reduce the amount of separate cabling and distribution equipment, some networks and stations use a system based on SMPTE standards for *embedded audio*. This system embeds up to 16 channels (eight pairs) of AES/EBU digital audio signals into the vertical interval data area of SD or HD digital video signals. They can then be carried through most parts of the video system together, without any separate audio switching or processing.

The disadvantage of an embedded audio system is that, whenever it is desired to change the audio (e.g., for editing or mixing new content), it is necessary to disembed the audio and then re-embed it again afterward. There are also problems when video is passed through devices such as DVEs, where, again, the audio has to be disembedded first.

Video Timing

The *timing* of video signals being mixed or switched is very important, particularly for analog video. If two analog video signals are switched from one to another when their sync pulses are not precisely aligned, this will result in a "bounce" or other disturbance in the output video signal when viewed on a picture monitor or receiver. If two nonsynchronized signals are mixed together, then the resulting picture will be distorted and may become unstable, and if the chrominance signals are not aligned within very small tolerances, color errors will result. Therefore, all signal sources in a studio are synchronized with a signal that comes from a common *sync pulse generator* (SPG), and the lengths of video cables for different sources feeding video switchers are carefully matched to maintain timing accuracy.

Where video signals come from remote sources, which cannot be synchronized, they are passed through a device called a *frame synchronizer*. This is able to store a whole frame of video and automatically adjusts its output timing to synchronize the signal with station video signals.

With digital video systems, the timing accuracy of signals arriving at a switcher is less critical than with analog, because the receiving device can accept digital signals with some degree of timing variations and still produce stable outputs. Nevertheless, all sources in a digital station are synchronized together to avoid timing problems building up, and frame synchronizers are still required for remote sources.

We mentioned earlier that a DVE unit delays a video signal by one complete frame. This generally is acceptable from a video timing point of view because the horizontal and vertical sync points repeat every frame, so the signal can still be switched, mixed, or recorded. It does, however, create a problem for *lip sync*, which we discuss later in the chapter. It may also cause some timing problems in systems still using analog video with color subcarrier.

Audio for Television

Audio systems and individual items of equipment used for television have many similarities to those used in radio, but there are some differences and additional considerations as described in the following sections.

Audio Production

A typical television studio setup often involves many more microphones and live audio sources than for radio. Studio microphones suitable for use in vision are used and, for some types of production, a long *microphone boom* may be used to locate a microphone near the action at high level but out of camera sight.

Wireless microphones are frequently used to allow artists to move around unencumbered by microphone cables. The artist wears a small radio transmitter, or it is built into the microphone itself; a receiving antenna and receiver away from the studio floor picks up the signal and feeds it to the audio mixing console.

The studio audio mixer output is recorded with the video on a videotape machine or server, rather than with an audio recorder. Dedicated audio workstations are not generally used in television, although hard disk audio recorders may be used for some sources and functions, such as sound effects.

Audio Editing and Post-production

Audio editing for television is usually combined with the video postproduction process. This may be in a video edit suite, using a conventional audio mixer, when sources from VTRs are played back and re-recorded to produce the finished program. Audio editing can also be carried out as part of the nonlinear video editing process, and such systems provide for separately mixing and processing the audio.

Audio Sweetening

The audio that was originally recorded with some programs often needs to be modified and enhanced. This is known as *audio sweetening* and is part of the postproduction process.

Surround Sound

As described in Chapter 15, DTV has the capability to carry surround sound audio. This requires production, network, and station facilities to have audio systems that can handle six channels of audio. In particular, audio mixers, monitoring, switching, and distribution systems, previously intended for stereo audio only, all have to be upgraded with provision for surround sound operations.

Dolby E

Distribution and recording of surround sound signals requires six channels of audio. This creates a problem because many VTRs have only two or four audio channels, and network distribution typically carries one stereo audio signal only. A system called *Dolby E*, developed by Dolby Laboratories, can be used to lightly compress up to eight audio channels into the bandwidth occupied by a single AES/EBU digital audio signal. This signal can then be recorded onto a single digital VTR or video server and can be distributed over an AES/EBU stereo audio channel from a production or postproduction facility to the network, and on to the broadcast station. There it can be converted back to individual audio channels for mixing and switching in master control, and finally re-encoded as AC-3 audio for transmission.

Audio Processing

The DTV audio system is able to carry a much wider dynamic range of audio than NTSC, so audio compression before encoding is not strictly necessary. In theory, the AC-3 decoder in the DTV receiver is able to carry out audio compression to suit the taste of the listener and the listening environment. In practice, some, but not all, stations do process DTV audio before AC-3 encoding, as shown in Figure 9.11 later in this chapter.

Audio-Video Synchronization

The term *audio-video synchronization* refers to the fact that the audio in a television program must match up—or be synchronized—with the video picture that accompanies it. Synchronization errors are particularly objectionable when people are speaking, so they are also known as *lip sync* errors (when a person's mouth movements do not correspond with the sound being heard).

Audio-video sync errors may be introduced whenever the audio signal is distributed or processed separately from the video. They may occur in many parts of the program chain, from production through to the receiver, and this applies in both analog and digital systems. There are, however, more ways in which errors may occur when using digital systems, and the errors can be much greater when problems occur. It is important that such errors should be prevented or corrected. If not, even small errors in several parts of the system can add up to significant and objectionable errors by the time they reach the viewer. This is not a trivial engineering task— a lot of effort is needed to maintain synchronization throughout the television distribution chain.

An example of a source of lip sync error is when a video signal is passed through a frame synchronizer. In that case, the video signal will be delayed by at least one frame or about 33 milliseconds. Errors may also be introduced when audio and video signals take different paths on a program link, say for a remote news contribution to a network or station, or when audio and video signals are edited separately in an edit suite or nonlinear editor.

Such errors can be corrected by inserting either audio or video delays into the system, to bring the signals back into synchronization. A delay is a device that takes the audio or video signal as an input and stores it for a period of time before sending it out. The complication is that the synchronization errors are often not constant (e.g., a video signal may sometimes pass through a DVE and sometimes not), so the compensating delay also needs to be adjusted. Even if a television studio is well synchronized internally, it is usually necessary to have additional adjustable delay units available, in case a signal being fed into the studio from outside is out of synchronization and needs to be corrected.

While there are differences of opinion, a commonly accepted rule for broadcasters is that audio signals should not be later than the video by about 60 milliseconds, nor earlier than about 30 milliseconds when seen by the final viewer at home, or the errors will be noticeable to many people. The delay can be larger when the audio is later, because that is the natural state of affairs seen in real life, since light waves travel much faster than sound through the air. Because there is some degree of uncertainty in audio-video timing caused by the DTV transmission process, broadcasters need to keep audio-video sync at the input to the ATSC encoding equipment at the studios to much tighter tolerances than this. The goal is to correct for zero lip sync error at each stage of the production and distribution process.

Ancillary Systems

Television studio requirements for ancillary systems such as clocks, timers, intercom, talkback, and on-air lights are very similar to those described for radio in Chapter 8. Obviously, the scale of such systems is usually larger, to cater for the increased size and complexity of most television facilities.

The station master clock is synchronized with a generator for SMPTE timecode, which is distributed to all equipment that needs a time reference. In this way, both staff and equipment in the station are working with exactly the same accurate time.

In the case of studio talkback, television systems include communications with camera operators and production staff on the studio floor, who wear headsets to communicate without interrupting the ongoing program.

Ingest and Conversion

Ingest

Program feeds come into a television network or station through various links and routes. These may include satellite and microwave radio links, fiber-optic cables, coaxial cables, and physical videotape delivery. The process of *ingest* includes checking material as it arrives, recording as necessary onto videotape or servers, and routing to the correct destinations for further processing or transmission.

Ingest Automation

Much of the ingest process may be controlled by an automation system. This keeps track of schedules for incoming programs from satellite links, where material is stored, what format conversion and so forth may be required, machines to use, and other necessary details.

File Transfers

Rather than sending material as audio and video signals in real time, many networks and stations are moving to systems that distribute program material as data files containing video, audio, and metadata (information about the program material). These are transported over private or public data networks, using Internet protocol, hence the process is often referred to as *video over IP*. The incoming files are ultimately stored on video servers.

As mentioned in the Video Servers section, the SMPTE MXF specifications standardize the interchange of program material as files, with great advantages for the broadcaster.

Format Conversion

In the United States, programs may be produced in standard definition, having about 480 active lines, or in one of the high definition formats, having 720 lines or 1080 lines. For various reasons, a network or station may wish to use a program in a different format from the one in which it was produced. For example, it may need to use an HD program on an NTSC channel, or as part of a standard definition multiplex, or incorporate some SD material as a segment in an HD program. In each case, a format converter is used to take the input signal and convert it to the required format using digital signal processing.

This process is referred to as *upconversion* when the number of lines is increased and *downconversion* when it is decreased. Upconverted SD pictures can never look as good as true HD material, but good quality can be produced if the original material comes from high-quality cameras and has passed only through a digital distribution chain.

With format conversion, the picture aspect ratio often has to be changed between 4:3 and 16:9. This requires decisions to be made on whether any of the picture will be cropped in this process, what size black bars (or other colors) will be added to the sides or top and bottom of the picture, and whether any anamorphic squeeze or stretch will be done to help fill the output frame with picture. Sometimes a combination of all these techniques may be used.

Standards Conversion

When television programs that were produced in accordance with one television standard, such as 625-line PAL, need to be used by a broadcaster with another transmission standard, such as 525-line NTSC, then the conversion is done with a *standards converter*. The process has some similarities to format conversion, but the big difference is that the picture frame rate has to be changed, typically from 25 frames per second to approximately 30 frames per second, or vice versa. Conversion between PAL, SECAM, and NTSC, in any direction, is frequently required for international program exchange.

Television Master Control

Master control contains the equipment for control of the on-air program, whether from a network release center, a station group centralcasting location, or a local station. System architecture for this function varies considerably for different networks and stations, and for NTSC or DTV station outputs, so what follows should be considered as an example only.

Figure 9.11, on page 175, illustrates in very simple terms how a master control system might be configured for a *local DTV station*. It shows various local and remote sources feeding a master control switcher. The video and audio outputs from this switcher then feed the ATSC video and audio encoders and multiplexer (audio processing at this point is optional), and the output goes to the transmitter. Arrangements for a *local analog station* output are similar, but without the ATSC video and audio encoders, and audio processing is essential.

Arrangements for a *network master control* may be similar, but the master control switcher output in that case will feed the encoders for the network or group distribution, and then go to a satellite uplink rather than a terrestrial transmitter. Arrangements for a station group *centralcasting master control* will have many of the same elements.

The simplified figure does not show any of the monitoring that is normally associated with a master control facility.

Sources

The principal local sources of video programming and advertisements are most likely one or more video servers. Figure 9.9 shows a large array of servers installed in a major network playout facil-

Figure 9.9. Server-Based Playout System
Courtesy of PBS and Omneon Video Networks

ity with multiple program feeds; local stations will be less elabor-
ate. Other sources may include VTRs, graphics systems, character
generators, an audio recorder, and a microphone for live announcements. One or more local studio outputs will also feed the master
control switcher.

Remote sources include the feed from the network and other
sources, perhaps a live sporting venue or remote truck. If the
station is producing a high definition output, but its local or remote
sources are in standard definition, then an upconverter is required
for the SD source material. It may also include the feed from a
group centralcasting location, which may be left permanently
selected during periods when the station service originates at the
central location.

There may well be more program sources than there are inputs on
the master control switcher, so it frequently works in conjunction
with an audio and video routing switcher, to make all the sources
available for selection on air.

Master Control Switcher

The master control switcher has some similarities to a production switcher, in that it has input selector buttons, one simple M/E unit, and usually a DVE. It also has key functions for adding graphics and captions to the broadcast program. An example of the control panel for a master control switcher is shown in Figure 9.10.

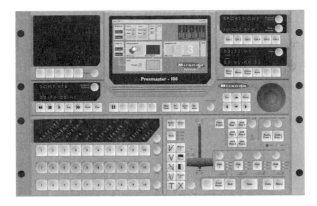

Figure 9.10. Master Control Switcher
Courtesy of Miranda

Differences from a production switcher are that it has audio inputs as well as video for each source and is able to switch them together, with an *audio-follow-video* function. It can also switch or mix separate audio sources for audio announcements or music. Some master control switchers have functions for starting VTRs or other machines when the source is selected.

When operated manually, a master control switcher works in *preset-take* mode. The operator preselects the next source using a push button on the *Preset* bus. At the time the switch is required, the *Take* button is pressed and the new source is switched to air. Transitions such as wipes and fades can also be executed on cue, together with effects such as *squeezeback*, using the DVE to allow an upcoming promo and so on to be shown with the end of the previous program. Captions and graphics can also be keyed over the program video, including the station logo and Emergency Alert System (EAS) text.

Audio announcements, either live or prerecorded, may be added using a *voice-over* facility, which drops the level of the main program to allow the announcement to be heard. The switcher may also make provision for inserting EAS audio in place of the program audio. There are outputs for feeding picture monitors for the preset and program signals and also for monitoring the audio. Audio level metering may be built in or provided externally.

This type of equipment is available to switch analog, SD digital, or HD digital signals. Where a station operates two separate outputs, one for NTSC and one for DTV, there may be two master control areas. Alternatively, one master control position may be able to control two switchers from the same control panel. Similarly, when a station operates several DTV program services for *multicasting* (see Chapter 15), the different outputs may be switched from one control panel, controlling several switchers.

Emergency Alert System Equipment

As noted in Chapter 8 on radio studios, EAS equipment must be installed somewhere in a broadcast station's air chain. In a radio station, this equipment is installed between the output of the on-air mixing board and the feed to the transmitter. In a local television station, the arrangements are similar but, in this case, the equipment must have the ability to interrupt both audio and video, or at least to interrupt the audio and insert a video text message over a portion of the normal picture. One arrangement for this is shown in Figure 9.11 on page 175. Here, the EAS audio output feeds the switcher, which switches that source to the output on demand. The EAS text output is fed to a character generator, which generates the video text, and this is keyed over part of the video screen. In an alternative arrangement, the EAS announcement switching may be carried out downstream from the master control switcher.

Time Delay

Master control for a network may feed several network distributions, intended for local stations in different time zones. Assuming the live network feed originates in the Eastern time zone, the others can be produced just by inserting a suitable delay. Traditionally, this was done by recording the output on a VTR and playing back the tape at a later time (known as *tape delay*). The current method is to use a video server, which records the live network feed and provides multiple outputs of the same material with different time delays. It can start replaying the delayed material while still recording the current program.

Master control in both network and station output feeds may need a smaller, switchable delay of several seconds to allow for deletion of profanity or undesirable content from live shows before it is sent to air. Although this task can be performed with a disk-based server, digital delay units are available for just this purpose, using solid-state memory.

Television Automation

On-Air Automation

Manual control of a master control switcher is possible for simple operations, but it gets very difficult for an operator to implement current network or station playout schedules. These are often a complex sequence of many segments for programs, advertisements, promos, and other material, that need to be switched on air at the right time, often in quick succession. The problems are compounded with a multitude of graphics, captions, and special effects to be controlled, and multiplied again if there is more than one output channel.

The use of automation to support the on-air master control process is, therefore, almost universal. It reduces on-air mistakes and ensures that advertisements are played out as scheduled, which is important since this is the source of revenue for a commercial station. The on-air automation system controls the local servers, VTRs, and other sources. It finds and cues program material using SMPTE timecode as the locator. It starts machines and controls the switcher that puts the source on air, initiates transitions and effects, and keys captions and graphics.

Playlist

The key to automation control is the *playlist*. This is based on the station program schedule and includes all the *events* that need to take place to produce the continuous program output from the station. Each event has a time entry indicating when it needs to take place. At the correct time, the automation system sends commands to the appropriate equipment (e.g., "Start" to a VTR) to initiate the action needed for the event.

The playlist is generated some time before transmission, taking input from the station *traffic* system, which is responsible for keeping track of what advertising has been sold, when it will be played out, and what all the segments are for the program schedule.

Other Automation Functions

It was mentioned previously that the process of ingest may be supported with an automation system. Automation may also be used to support other aspects of media preparation, keeping track of what material is available, and where it is stored. The electronic newsroom system also uses automation, both for content ingest and playout.

Integrating these systems with the on-air playout system, or at least having links to allow them to share information, minimizes the need for manual intervention and reduces the likelihood of errors throughout the system.

With some station groups, there may be a centralcasting function that involves centralized management of the station automation system, with some content being downloaded to the station and played out from a local server under automation control, rather than complete assembly of the program at the central location. Arrangements may vary considerably and are outside the scope of this book.

ATSC Encoding

In Chapter 15 we explain how digital video and audio has to be compressed and combined into a single *transport stream* before it

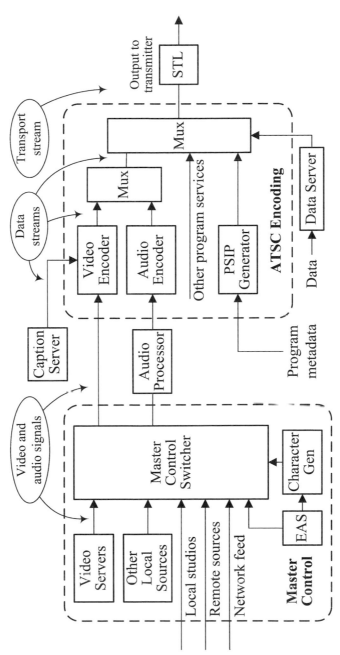

Figure 9.11. DTV Master Control and Emission Encoding

can be transmitted. This is necessary because the data rates of the video and audio signals that come from the video server, or other sources, are far higher than can be transmitted in the ATSC bitstream.

As shown in Figure 9.11, the video compression is carried out in an *ATSC encoder*, also known as an MPEG-2 encoder, and the audio compression is carried out in an *AC-3 encoder*. Each encoder produces a data stream called an *elementary stream*, which are combined into a single stream of data packets in a *multiplexer* or *mux*. The output of this multiplexer is then combined, in a second multiplexer, with other packets of information (see following sections), to produce the final *transport stream* that can be fed to the transmitter.

Depending on the equipment design, the multiplexers may be separate devices or may be in a single integrated box with the video encoder. The AC-3 encoder may be combined in the integrated unit or may be a stand-alone device.

Most stations locate the ATSC encoding equipment at the studio center and feed the single transport stream over the *studio-transmitter link* (STL) to the transmitter. However, in the early days of DTV, for simplicity in getting on air, some stations decided to locate the ATSC encoder at the transmitter site, simply feeding it with the same video and audio as that fed to the NTSC transmitter. This second arrangement has several disadvantages for the DTV service and is not practical to implement with high definition video. It will become less common as the DTV transition progresses.

Multicasting Operations

Figure 9.11 shows the basic station output arrangement for a single DTV program service. However, many stations multicast two or more program services in a single output bitstream on their DTV channel. In that case, there will be multiple video and audio feeds from master control, and multiple video and audio encoders. These other program services are all combined in the final mux, as indicated in the figure.

Closed Captioning Equipment

The FCC requires most programming to be transmitted with *closed captioning*. This allows a viewer with a hearing disability to display a text version of the spoken audio, when the program is displayed on a television set.

It is outside the scope of this book to cover exactly how closed captions are generated, but most programs one received from the network or other supplier with caption information carried along with the video signal, although not visible. Live local programs, such as news, have to be captioned at the station, although the person producing the captions can, in fact, be located off-site and after provides the service remotely.

As discussed in Chapter 14, with NTSC the closed captioning data is carried in line 21 of the *vertical blanking interval* (VBI), and no special action is required for transmission. The situation is somewhat more complex for DTV. While the caption information may be carried *embedded* in the digital version of the VBI in the studio center, that part is not encoded for transmission. Therefore, the caption information has to be extracted and placed in the *User Bits* part of the encoded *video bitstream*. This process may take place entirely inside the encoder, or may require an external device, called a *caption server*, as shown in Figure 9.11. The caption server is also needed if DTV captions are being generated locally.

PSIP Generator

Program and System Information Protocol (PSIP, see Chapter 15) tables are produced in a computer called a *PSIP generator*. The output of this is a data stream, which feeds into the ATSC multiplexer or ATSC encoder (if they are combined together in one unit), as shown in Figure 9.11. The PSIP generator is usually connected through a network with other computers, such as the *traffic system*, and *automation system*, which produce and manage the program schedule and associated information. This information, known as *metadata*, is needed to help generate the PSIP tables. An ATSC standard called *Programming Metadata Communication Protocol* (PMCP) enables it to be shared among different systems and equipment.

Data Broadcasting Equipment

For DTV stations, a *datacasting* service (see Chapter 15) may be combined with the television programs in the DTV *multiplexer* at the output of the studios, as shown in Figure 9.11.This requires a data connection to the ATSC multiplexer or ATSC encoder (if they are combined together in one unit) from the *data server*. The data server stores and communicates the data service and is usually connected through a network with other computers, either at the station or elsewhere, which produce and manage the data information.

Bitstream Distribution and Splicing

The previous sections on master control and ATSC encoding for a DTV service assume that the program feed from the network is converted to uncompressed *baseband* video and audio before being distributed at the station, switched to air through a master control switcher, and then ATSC encoded for transmission.

Not all networks and stations follow this model, however. In an alternative system architecture, the network carries out the ATSC encoding for the network DTV program feed (usually, but not necessarily, in high definition) at the network release center. It then sends the much lower data rate compressed transport stream through the network distribution (usually a satellite link) to local stations. This produces considerable savings in satellite circuit costs and helps maintain quality by reducing the number of times the network signal has to be encoded and decoded. This network feed is effectively ready for transmission at the station, after it has local PSIP information added.

With this arrangement, the local station prepares its own local material as previously described and encodes it with its own ATSC encoder. However, whenever a switch is required from local to network material, this is done by means of a *bitstream splicer*, which switches seamlessly between the local and network bitstreams. Special arrangements are made for inserting the local station logo on the network feed without decoding the compressed stream.

It is possible for control of the bitstream splicer to be integrated into a master control switcher for the local sources, and controlled from the station automation, so there is no overall increase in operational complexity.

Compressed Bitstream Distribution

Compressed bitstreams are distributed within the station using similar techniques to serial digital video. There are two main standards for this: SMPTE 310M, which is used mainly for the connection from the multiplexer to the STL, and DVB-ASI (Digital Video Broadcasting Asynchronous Serial Interface), which is usually used everywhere else.

Bitstream Recording

The ATSC encoded transport stream can be recorded on a *bitstream server*. Thus, the ATSC-encoded feed from a network may be recorded in this form and played back at any time for transmission. This is a very efficient method of recording HD signals for transmission, but it is not practical for production or postproduction.

Mezzanine-Level Distribution

In addition to the "uncompressed" or "fully compressed ready for transmission" architectures, there is a third alternative. This is based on an intermediate, more lightly compressed bitstream, sometimes known as *mezzanine level*, typically 45 Mbps, which is what many networks use for their DTV network distribution. Many servers also record a lightly compressed bitstream, of various formats. Currently, most stations decode these signals back to uncompressed baseband video and audio for distribution in the station. It is, however, possible to distribute the mezzanine-level signals in the station, with yet another possible system architecture. Details of this process are beyond the scope of this book.

Internet Streaming

When a broadcaster wishes to create a stream of the station's video or audio for Internet distribution, the stream may be produced by the station, using a suitable streaming encoder. Alternatively, the broadcaster may provide a regular audio and video program feed to a third-party organization that provides all the facilities and management needed for streaming encoding, together with the Web servers and interface to the Internet.

In either case, the station may use a feed from the same master switcher that feeds the broadcast transmitter, or may perhaps generate a second independent feed, which allows for dropping or adding Internet-specific programming or advertisements.

CHAPTER 10

Remote Broadcasting

Remote broadcasting covers production, or acquisition of program material, in locations away from the studio center. News is an important part of radio and television broadcasting, and television, in particular, relies greatly on production that takes place outside the studio, for sports, music events, and drama production.

The acquisition systems for news and other remote production activities are described in this chapter, while the link systems for getting them back to the studio are covered in Chapter 11.

Radio News Gathering

Radio news gathering (acquisition) includes reporting from the field, recording interviews, press conferences, and so on, and transporting them back to studio centers for incorporating into news programs. Most equipment for radio news acquisition uses the same principles as fixed radio studio equipment. However, the emphasis is on portability, ruggedness, and ease of use in difficult conditions. Microphones are normally highly directional and may have windshields to reduce the effect of wind noise on the microphone diaphragm. Recorders are often small enough to be held in the hand and may use tape cassette, MiniDisc, or, increasingly, solid-state flash memory, with both microphone and line-level inputs. An example of a solid-state flash memory recorder is shown in Figure 10.1. Recorders may have two or more inputs, or a small external mixer may be used for multiple sources. Monitoring is on headphones, and battery power is essential for all equipment.

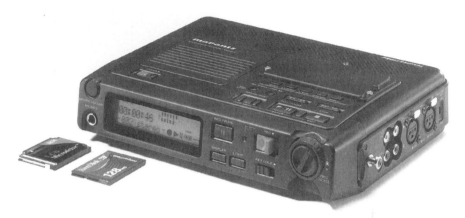

Figure 10.1. Portable Compact Flash Recorder
Courtesy of Marantz

When covering press conferences, a common audio feed is often provided from the podium microphones, which is split and distributed for use by multiple reporters.

Recorded media may be transported back to the studio for editing, or live contributions may be sent over contribution links of various types, as described in Chapter 11. When on remote assignments, some reporters may take a portable mixer and more than one recorder to allow them to edit a report in the field, before sending it to the station. It is also possible to transfer audio files from a digital recorder to a laptop computer and edit the material there. At the other extreme, the simplest live arrangement is the reporter speaking over a regular telephone line or cell phone.

Cue Audio

Wherever possible, the audio sent to a remote contribution site for cue purposes is a *mix-minus* feed from the audio mixer (i.e., the output of the studio, minus the contribution audio). This helps avoid problems with audio feedback and makes two-way communication with presenters and talent possible.

The reporter may also have a portable receiver for listening to the station output off-air. This gives the reporter an indication of what is going out, but preferably should not be used for cue purposes.

Radio Remote Production

Radio remote productions include live or recorded programming such as sporting events, concerts, promotional events at county fairs and other shows from outside the studio. Facilities required may range from simple to complex.

Equipment is usually transported in carrying cases in a small truck and may include portable or smaller versions of equipment used in the studio of the following types:

- Microphones, headphones, headsets (combined mic and headphone)
- Audio mixer
- CD players
- DAT, MiniDisc, and Compact Flash recorders
- Monitor loudspeakers

Other equipment that may be needed for some types of remote events includes the following:

- Wireless microphones
- Public address amplifier and speakers

For live broadcasts, some of the same equipment as listed for news reporting may be used for communicating with the studio, and in addition the following may be needed:

- Remote pickup (RPU) radio link system
- Portable antenna system for RPU

Television News Gathering

Electronic news gathering (ENG) forms an important part of broadcast station operations. As with radio, most of the equipment uses essentially the same principles as fixed television studio equipment. However, the emphasis is even more on portability, ruggedness, and ease of use in difficult conditions, compared to equivalent TV studio equipment.

ENG news crews and their equipment may be transported in a small truck or wagon or may work with a larger truck that includes a microwave link or a satellite uplink for live communications with the studio.

Cameras and Recorders

ENG cameras all have built-in recorders, so the term *camcorder* is often used. Most of the small VTR formats have been used at one time or another. Principal formats used today include BetacamSP, DVCPRO, DVCPRO50, and DV. The new generation XDCAM (optical disk) and P2 (solid-state) recorders are intended primarily for ENG and EFP applications and are likely to be widely adopted. Figure 10.2 shows an example of a portable camera with a built-in P2 solid-state recorder.

Figure 10.2. Portable Camera
Courtesy of Panasonic

At the time of writing this book, only a small number of stations are producing news in high definition and equipping their news crews with HD camcorders. That situation may change as the migration to DTV continues and the cost of HD equipment continues to fall.

Cameras are usually handheld (actually shoulder-mounted) but may be used on a tripod, with a pan-and-tilt head, or installed in a vehicle or helicopter, where a gyro-stabilized mount is required to produce stable pictures. The crew may have a portable lighting kit to supplement available light where necessary.

Recorded media may be transported back to the studio for editing. Alternatively, live contributions or recordings may be sent to the studio over contribution links of various types.

Cue Feed

For live contributions, a cue audio and video feed from the studio is required to allow the reporter to speak when required and/or converse with the studio staff. With NTSC transmission, this cue feed is often taken from the station off-air signal, using the Pro subcarrier channel for audio (see the Audio Signal section in Chapter 14). With DTV transmission, it is not possible to use the off-air signal for cue purposes, since there is no equivalent of the Pro channel, and the main program audio has a significant coding/decoding delay. So, when NTSC transmissions come to an end, other arrangements will have to be made. Either ENG links will need to be made bidirectional in order to provide a return path or another return link method will need to be established. In the mean time, communications are usually established with mobile radios and cell phones.

Field Editing

Ultra-compact editing facilities are available and may be taken on assignment to edit and assemble stories while in the field. An example of a portable two-deck DVCPRO format VTR editor is shown in Figure 10.3. Material may also be digitized and transferred to a laptop computer for editing in the field.

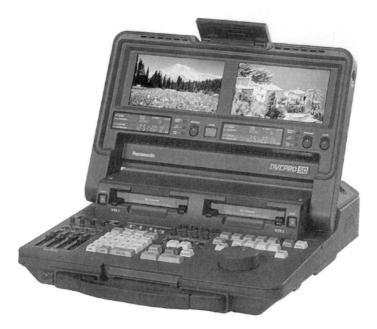

Figure 10.3. Portable Editor
Courtesy of Panasonic

ENG trucks equipped with microwave or satellite links may also be equipped with basic editing machines or have equipment to allow material to be reviewed before sending to the studio.

Television Remote Production

Remote field production falls into two main categories: (1) electronic field production (EFP) with portable equipment and (2) mobile production relying on equipment installed in mobile vehicles.

Electronic Field Production

EFP normally uses portable self-contained equipment that can be transported in rugged shipping cases. Sometimes, however, EFP equipment may be installed in a small truck or van, so the distinc-

microphones, and other feeds in and out of the truck are made on a special connection panel in a compartment that is shielded from the weather.

Equipment types in the vehicle, including switchers, monitors, VTRs, servers, audio console, communications systems, and so on, are all much the same as those used in studios.

Slow-Motion Cameras

Special cameras are available to help produce high-quality slow-motion pictures, especially for action replays in sports programming. Slow-motion playback requires more frames than are recorded for a normal speed motion. Therefore, when a conventional camera is used, frames have to be repeated upon playback, resulting in jerky motion. A slow-motion camera works at a higher frame rate, and more frames can be recorded on an associated hard disk recorder. This enables much smoother motion when played back at slower speeds. A special controller is used for slow-motion replay, which provides rapid access to particular parts of the action and controls the playback speed and other functions.

CHAPTER 11
Links

Program links fall into three main categories as follows:

- *Contribution links* for sending news contributions and other remote production material to a network or studio center
- *Network distribution links* for distributing network program feeds to multiple locations around the country
- *Studio-transmitter links* (STLs) for connecting a station studio center to its transmitter site

Several types of links are used for each category for radio and television, based on different technologies. This gets to be a complex subject, so we will only deal with the main principles here.

Contribution Links for Radio

Telephone Line

Standard telephone lines are probably the easiest links to set up, and therefore are often used for news reporting. Figure 11.1 shows a simple analog audio mixer combined with a telephone interface unit. This unit works with a standard dial-up phone line to connect a remote location to the studio, and provides reasonable quality mono audio with a return audio cue feed. Similar interface devices are also used that work with cell phones.

More sophisticated devices are available that process the audio in special ways to improve the sound quality. Some of them use more than one phone line to provide more bandwidth.

Figure 11.1. Audio Mixer/Telephone Interface
Courtesy of JK Audio

ISDN Line

Integrated Services Digital Network (ISDN) is a special type of digital phone line. Using a special codec at each end of the line, full-range broadcast-quality stereo audio can be carried.

Remote Pickup

Remote pickup units (RPUs) use radio transmissions with various frequencies allocated in the HF, VHF, and UHF bands. These provide reasonably good-quality mono analog contribution links without needing a phone line. An RPU has a transmitter with a directional antenna at the remote site—usually mounted on a van or truck, although it can be a portable unit. It sends analog audio back to the studio, where an antenna is usually mounted on the roof or tower at the studio, with the receiver in the master control area.

T1 Line

A T1 line is a digital data circuit with a bandwidth of 1.544 Mbps. It may be leased from a telecommunications service provider or implemented as part of a broadband microwave system, set up for other purposes. Full-range broadcast-quality stereo audio can be transmitted using special codecs (coder/decoders) at each end of the line, with full-quality feeds in both directions.

LAN/WAN

Program contributions may be received as audio files distributed over a computer network. The network may be a virtual private network established over the Internet or may be set up on private data circuits leased from a telecommunications service provider.

Contribution Links for Television

Microwave

The most common television contribution links use microwave radios, with frequencies allocated in the high UHF and SHF bands. Microwaves have extremely short wavelengths that must have line-of-sight transmission. So the transmitting antenna, with a parabolic-shape reflector, is raised as high as possible on a telescopic mast, to get line of sight to a receive antenna mounted as high as possible at the studio center. A station may set up a central ENG receive point, possibly their transmitter tower or another high point in town, from where the signal is retransmitted to the studios.

At the remote site, such equipment is usually mounted on an electronic news gathering (ENG) truck, as shown in Figure 11.2. The truck also provides transport for the camera crew and equipment and usually has an electrical generator so it is self-contained.

Upon arrival at the news site, the link equipment operator raises the antenna mast and aims the microwave transmitting antenna in the direction of the studio, where the microwave receive antenna is located. For a live story, the video output of the camera and the

Figure 11.2. ENG Microwave Truck
Courtesy of Frontline Communications

sound mixer audio are fed to the microwave transmitter. If the story is prerecorded, either the camera replay output is fed to the link, or the camera tape may be replayed from a player in the truck.

It is also possible to use a microwave link with a helicopter being used for live ENG, in which case a stabilized steerable antenna is required to maintain the line-of-site link to the ground receive point.

Microwave links can carry both analog and digital audio and video signals. ENG links for DTV are available using COFDM modulation (see Chapter 4) to provide a very robust signal. There must be good coordination between all operators of ENG microwave equipment in a given geographical area to ensure that each microwave link does not interfere with any other in the region.

Satellite

Microwave links to the station do not work for all locations where news may occur. To allow live reporting over a larger area, TV networks and some stations use *satellite news gathering* (SNG). This refers to the satellite link used for sending the signal to the studio. An example of an SNG truck, with the *uplink* dish antenna, is shown in Figure 11.3.

Figure 11.3. SNG Uplink Truck
Courtesy of Frontline Communications

The signal from the satellite is received at the station (or wherever else it is needed) with a satellite downlink. Various frequencies in the SHF band are allocated for these links.

Network Distribution Links for Radio and Television

Satellite

The majority of radio and television networks and syndication program services are uplinked to a geostationary satellite. Signals are received at the station with earth station downlink antennas of a type similar to that shown in Figure 11.4. As for SNG, various frequencies in the SHF band are allocated.

Figure 11.4. Satellite Downlink Antenna
Courtesy of Patriot Antenna Systems

LAN/WAN

Network programming that is not for live broadcast may be received as audio or video files distributed over a computer network, as also applies for contribution links.

Studio-Transmitter Links for Radio and Television

The STL is the means by which program material produced in the studio facility is transported to the transmitter site for broadcast. If the station's transmitter is located adjacent to its studios, then the

STL might simply be a cable, or set of cables, connecting the output from master control to the transmitter area. More often, however, the transmitter is located at a remote location, such as the top of a mountain or tall building. In that case, there are several different methods for transporting the program signal, as described in the following sections.

Leased Telephone Lines

One traditional means of getting radio program signals material to the transmitter is to use leased telephone lines. The local telephone company may be able to provide broadcast-quality links between studios and transmitters so that the broadcaster can feed the program audio signals into a telephone company–provided box at the studio facility and retrieve them from a telephone company terminal at the transmitter facility.

ISDN Line

ISDN lines, as discussed under Contribution Links, can also be used as a radio STL, although because of the cost of rental, they are often used as a backup to a primary microwave link.

T1 Line

A T1 line, as discussed under Contribution Links, is suitable as a radio STL, assuming that it is possible to get the wideband connection to the remote transmitter site. It may be leased from a telecommunications service provider or implemented as part of a broadband microwave system.

Microwave Links

Microwave STLs may be used for both radio and television, based on the same principle as television ENG contribution links. In this case, they will have a fixed microwave transmitter and antenna at each end of the link. Because microwave transmissions work only with direct line-of-sight, the transmitting antenna must have a good "view" of the receiving antenna at the transmitter site. If an obstruction is unavoidable, sometimes a *multihop* link is installed, with a microwave receiver and second transmitter at an intermediate location that can see both the studios and transmitter sites.

Examples of typical microwave antennas on a tower are shown in Figure 11.5. With fixed links, the actual radio transmitter and receiver equipment is often located in a building adjacent to the

Figure 11.5. Microwave Link Antennas
Courtesy of Microwave Radio Communications

tower, connected to the antenna with a feed-line. This type of link is widely used both for radio and television. They are available with the wide bandwidth needed for video signals, and are good for linking to the remote mountaintop locations where FM and television transmitters are frequently located.

Fiber-Optic Links

In some locations it may be possible to run a fiber-optic cable from the studio facility to the transmitter site. This can provide an excellent high-quality bidirectional link for both audio and video. A special codec at each end of the fiber combines the various signals to be sent on a single fiber.

Fiber-optic cable consists of a long, thin strand of glass, sheathed in plastic, possibly with multiple fibers in each sheath. A beam of special light, from a laser, is modulated with the digital signals to be carried, in a multiplexed arrangement. The light enters the fiber at one end and undergoes repeated *total internal reflection*, which allows it to propagate for very long distances with negligible loss, and no distortion, and is detected by the receiver at the other end. Loss in the cable is extremely low, and transmission distances of many miles are possible. The other huge advantage of fiber-optic cable is that the light signals are completely unaffected by electrical and magnetic interference.

There are two varieties of fiber-optic cable: single-mode and multi-mode, which relate to the way the light is reflected inside the strand of glass. Single-mode is generally more expensive but is required for longer distances.

Analog and Digital Systems

Regardless of what path the signal takes for the link (e.g., simple cable, phone line, leased phone line, radio link, microwave link, satellite link), one other important characteristic must be considered—whether the link carries analog or digital signals.

The trend in broadcasting is toward digital signals throughout the chain, but the choice of codec technology and system will depend very much on the signal formats of the audio and video signals that are to feed the STL and that are needed for the transmitter site equipment. If necessary, *analog-to-digital* (A/D) and *digital-to-analog* (D/A) *converters* may be used to make the interfaces work.

Compressed Links

One important consideration for digital links is the data rate of the signal to be carried and the bandwidth that the link can handle. In some cases, audio and video data compression is used in conjunction with the link to reduce the data rate (see Chapter 15 for more on compression).

Links for DTV

Special arrangements are made for the various links needed for DTV. In particular, stations need to feed the ATSC bitstream while continuing to feed the NTSC transmitter, but often no further microwave frequencies are available. Digital equipment is available that combines the NTSC and ATSC signals together in a package that can be sent in the bandwidth of one channel.

TRANSMISSION STANDARDS
AND SYSTEMS

Sidebands and Bandwidth

In AM broadcasting, when the modulating signal (the audio program) is combined with the carrier, the varying amplitude RF signal that results is made up of the original carrier frequency and additional frequencies known as the upper and lower *sidebands* (see Chapter 4). For example, if the audio signal has frequencies extending to 10 kHz, then the sidebands will extend from the carrier frequency minus about 10 kHz and the carrier frequency plus about 10 kHz. This means they take up at least 20 kHz of radio spectrum. In reality, transmitters also produce additional energy in sidebands extending beyond these limits; this is sometimes referred to as *splatter*.

Because AM channels are allocated frequencies only 10 kHz apart, the transmission from an AM station extends into adjacent channels both above and below its allocated frequency. The maximum RF emission bandwidth allowed is specified by the FCC but, almost inevitably, first and second adjacent AM channels cannot be used in the same transmission area (factors affecting interference also include transmitted power and antenna directional characteristics).

Emissions Masks

Figure 12.1 shows the AM and FM band *emissions masks* defined by the FCC to protect other stations operating on nearby channels from interference. The emissions mask is the limit placed on the signal strength of the broadcast signal, and it is defined over a range of frequencies surrounding the carrier frequency. A broadcast station's signal strength at specific frequencies must decrease as the frequencies become farther away from the carrier, and the − 25 dB (decibel) figure, as shown, defines how much the reduction must be.

As Figure 12.1 illustrates, the radio spectrum available to an AM station (about 20 kHz) for its main signal is approximately 10 percent of that available to an FM station (about 240 kHz).

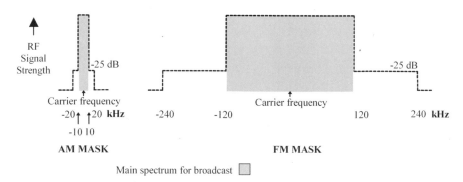

Figure 12.1. Comparison of AM and FM Band Emissions Masks

Subsidiary Communications for AM

An AM station's program material occupies all or most of the radio spectrum assigned to the station. This makes it extremely difficult to place a subcarrier for additional services in the channel, as used for FM stations (see following section).

Therefore, another method may be used for *multiplexing* (i.e., combining together) two signals in an AM broadcast channel. *Quadrature amplitude modulation* (QAM) has been used for many years as a means of allowing AM broadcasters to transmit auxiliary information on the main carrier frequency by varying another parameter of the carrier signal called *phase* (see Chapter 4 for more on QAM).

FM Transmission

In transmissions using FM—*frequency modulation*—the program audio signal is used to modulate the frequency of the carrier wave that will be transmitted by the station. When the amplitude of the program signal is zero, the carrier remains unmodulated. As the instantaneous amplitude of the program signal increases up to its maximum, then the carrier frequency varies accordingly, up to the maximum amount allowed, which is 100 percent modulation.

FM services are very robust and immune to interference from outside sources of RF. This is because, although interfering signals may add or subtract from the amplitude of the RF carrier, they do not affect the frequency of the wanted signal that carries the audio information heard at the receiver.

As mentioned previously, the bandwidth allocated to FM channels is much wider than AM, and this allows the bandwidth of the audio signal that can be transmitted to extend to about 15 kHz. This good frequency response, combined with good *signal-to-noise* ratio and low interference, makes FM capable of high-quality audio.

Carriers and Channels for FM

For FM broadcasting, the range of RF frequencies is 88 to 108 MHz in the very high frequency (VHF) band. Carriers are assigned to channels, which for FM are spaced at 200 kHz intervals in the United States (other countries use either 100 kHz or 200 kHz spacing), with the carrier frequency in the center of each channel.

Deviation, Sidebands, and Bandwidth

The change in frequency of the carrier, as it is modulated, is known as the *deviation*, or *frequency swing*. The maximum deviation allowed for 100 percent modulation is specified by the FCC as plus and minus 75 kHz.

Because it is the frequency, and not the amplitude, of the carrier that is varied, FM produces sidebands in a different way from AM. Without going into details, the modulating signal produces a range of upper and lower sidebands, extending much more than plus or minus 75 kHz from the carrier frequency. When using subcarriers, as discussed later, the sidebands extend out further than for mono audio alone. As Figure 12.1 illustrates, the radio spectrum available for the main signal from an FM station is specified by the FCC as plus or minus 120 kHz from the carrier frequency.

Because FM channels are allocated at 200 kHz spacing, the trans-mitted signal from an FM station therefore extends to some extent

into adjacent channels both above and below its allocated frequency. The maximum RF emission bandwidth allowed is specified by the FCC and is reduced for much of the adjacent channels.
To reduce interference, however, first adjacent FM channels are not
usually allocated for use in the same transmission area.

Stereo Coding

Two-channel stereo sound, consisting of left and right program
channels, is used almost universally at analog FM radio and TV
broadcast stations. A system of transmitting stereo over AM was
developed and incorporated into the FCC's rules. However,
because of increased potential for interference with other stations
and the generally poorer audio performance of AM, the system was
not widely adopted. Few AM stations these days transmit in
stereo.

No matter what type of analog broadcast station is involved (FM,
AM, or TV), all stereo broadcast systems use a method for coding
the left and right audio channels that ensures that the stereo signal
can be decoded and played by both stereophonic and monophonic
receivers. It is not sufficient to simply transmit a left channel signal
and a right channel signal. Instead, a "main program" channel
must be transmitted that combines both the left and right audio
signals together so it can be used by a monophonic receiver, and a

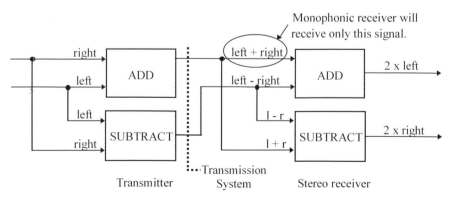

Figure 12.2. Stereo Coding

"stereo program" channel must be transmitted that can be coupled with the main program channel to produce left and right program material at a stereo receiver.

Figure 12.2 illustrates the method used to achieve this result. Before transmission, the left and right channels are added together to produce a combined mono *sum* signal (left + right), and the right channel signal is subtracted from the left to produce the supplementary stereo *difference* signal (left − right). After passing through the transmission system, the "left + right" signal can be received by mono receivers and played over a single loudspeaker. At a stereo receiver, the sum and difference signals are added together, and subtracted from each other, as follows:

	Addition				Subtraction		
	L	+	R		L	+	R
plus	L	−	R	minus	L	−	R
	2L		0		0		2R

This produces the original individual left and right channel signals (actually twice the amplitude, but that is easily adjusted), which can be played over stereo loudspeakers or headphones.

The stereo coding process is carried out using a *stereo generator*. Whether we are talking about an analog FM or TV station, the transmitter is only able to accept one audio signal to be modulated; therefore, the stereo generator has also to combine the sum and difference signals together in a special way, as described next. This system for broadcasting stereo sound is known as the *Zenith system* because it was developed by the Zenith Radio Corporation.

Stereo Signal Generation

In the case of FM radio, the stereo generator produces a composite output signal as shown in Figure 12.3. The "left + right" main program signal needed for mono reception is baseband audio, with

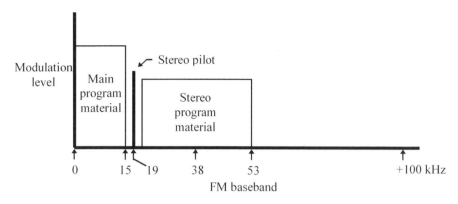

Figure 12.3. Composite FM Stereo Signal

15 kHz bandwidth. A *stereo pilot* tone of 19 kHz is added as a reference signal, and the "left – right" stereo difference signal needed
to produce the stereo channels is amplitude modulated onto the
38 kHz *second harmonic* of the 19 kHz stereo pilot (i.e., a subcarrier
at twice the frequency). Because the stereo difference signal is an
audio signal with 15 kHz bandwidth, the modulated subcarrier has
lower and upper sidebands, carrying the program information,
which extend 15 kHz below to 15 kHz above the *suppressed* 38 kHz
subcarrier. This whole composite stereo signal, which is still at
baseband, is fed to the FM transmitter.

The arrangement for analog TV is similar but with a different stereo
pilot frequency.

Although all combined together, these different signals do not
interfere with each other because they have different frequencies.
This also means that a stereo receiver can easily separate the signals
out again for decoding. A mono radio receiver may not be able to
separate out the stereo subcarrier signal from the mono signal, but
this is not important because the stereo signal is near the top of the
range of human hearing and is not reproduced by the receiver.

The stereo pilot mentioned earlier is an unmodulated subcarrier
(i.e., a subcarrier that does not have any additional information
added to it). One purpose of the stereo pilot is to provide a refer-

ence frequency for demodulating the stereo subcarrier. It also tells receivers that the host FM or analog TV station is broadcasting in stereo. If an FM or analog television station does not transmit the stereo pilot signal, then receivers will assume that the station is broadcasting a monaural program, and they will not try to decode the received audio into a left and right channel.

Subcarriers

As well as stereo audio, other subcarriers can be used to carry additional information in a broadcast signal, which may not be associated with the broadcaster's main programming. The following discussion about subcarriers uses the FM baseband signal for illustrative purposes. However, this explanation of how subcarriers are added to FM signals is equally applicable to analog TV aural (sound) signals.

A *subcarrier* is a special type of carrier. It has similar characteristics, except that it must first be added to a host carrier before the combined signal is modulated in the transmitter in order to be delivered to a receiver. Subcarriers are common in FM radio and analog TV systems because there is plenty of room in the channel for them to be added.

Figure 12.3 illustrates the fact that an FM stereo signal actually occupies only a little more than half of the baseband spectrum that can be used. The excess channel capacity that remains presents an opportunity for FM broadcasters to generate additional income by leasing out some, or all, of their excess channel capacity to third parties for subcarrier services such as background music, radio paging, or the Radio Reading Service. The same is true for TV broadcasters, although the subcarrier space available to them is slightly different than the subcarrier space available to FM stations. The FCC refers to these as *subsidiary communications authorization* (SCA) services.

The three most common FM band subcarriers in use today, apart from the 38 kHz stereo subcarrier, are the 57 kHz (RDS), 67 kHz, and 92 kHz subcarriers, as shown in Figure 12.4.

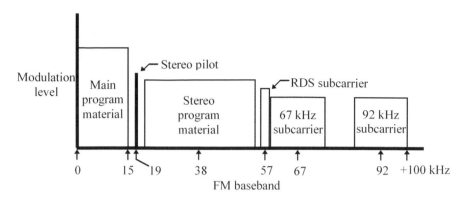

Figure 12.4. FM Stereo Signal with 57 kHz (RDS), 67 kHz, and 92 kHz Subcarriers

Radio Data System

In 1993, the National Radio Systems Committee (NRSC) adopted a standard for transmitting digital data at 1187.5 bits per second on a subcarrier in the FM baseband. This standard is called the *United States Radio Broadcast Data System* (RBDS), often referred to as RDS, for *Radio Data System*. Updated editions of this standard were adopted by the NRSC in 1998 and 2004.

The RDS signal carries data such as station identification, song titles, artist names, and other program-related information; it can also accommodate other text such as weather and traffic updates. RDS data can be displayed as scrolling text on a receiver's display panel.

The RDS subcarrier is centered on 57 kHz, the third harmonic of 19 kHz (the FM stereo pilot frequency), and the recommended bandwidth is approximately 4 kHz. As shown in Figure 12.4, the RDS signal fits between the stereo program material and the 67 kHz subcarrier.

CHAPTER 13

IBOC Digital Radio

In-Band, On-Channel (IBOC) digital radio is a new radio technology that is currently being deployed in the United States, whereby a digital signal is combined with the signal from an analog station. The name IBOC indicates that the digital service shares the same band and channel as the analog service. The AM and FM band IBOC systems being deployed in the United States, called HD Radio, were developed by iBiquity Digital Corporation. Following a rigorous evaluation by the National Radio Systems Committee (NRSC), completed in early 2002, the FCC in October 2002 approved HD Radio technology for use under an interim authorization. This allows FM broadcasters to transmit IBOC 24/7 but restricts AM transmissions to daytime-only use. At the time of this action, very little technical information was available about how AM IBOC would perform at night in the more difficult *skywave* propagation environment (see Chapter 17 for more on propagation).

In the first part of 2003, iBiquity made some changes to the specifications for the audio compression system, and stations started to broadcast using the new audio codec (called HDC) later in 2003. The FCC issued a Further Notice of Proposed Rulemaking and Notice of Inquiry on IBOC in April 2004. This sought comments on various questions related to IBOC deployment, and the industry replied with generally constructive and positive inputs. The next logical step in this process will be for the FCC to issue final rules on IBOC implementation.

The HD Radio system provides stereo digital audio services using the same frequencies as existing AM and FM radio stations. There are two versions of IBOC—for AM and FM. They provide similar capabilities, although the technical details vary. Characteristics that are common to both systems are described as follows.

Phased IBOC Introduction

IBOC is designed to be introduced in two phases—*hybrid* and *all-digital*—enabling a smooth evolution from the current analog services.

Hybrid Phase

The initial *hybrid* phase adds a digital service to the existing analog service, with identical audio programming (i.e., simulcasting) and some optional data services (which may include additional audio channels). This provides simultaneous analog and digital services to the same principal coverage area. Because the digital portion of the IBOC signal is at a much lower power level than the analog portion, as listeners approach the edge of the coverage area, the digital signal becomes unusable, and the IBOC receiver at that point *blends* from the digital to the analog signal. This avoids the abrupt reception failure that would otherwise occur (the so-called *cliff effect*).

During the hybrid phase, listeners may continue to use their existing receivers for the analog audio service or may purchase digital receivers for the digital audio and new data services. The new digital units can receive stations that are transmitting analog-only services, as well as those with IBOC services, which, as just mentioned, may blend from analog to digital depending upon signal reception conditions.

All-Digital Phase

At some point in the future, when IBOC receiver penetration is sufficient, broadcasters will be in a position to implement the *all-digital* phase. At that time, the analog signal will be turned off and the digital signal enlarged (but still within the FCC mask). This maximizes the coverage area and will provide capacity for additional data services. Currently, the FCC does not allow broadcasters to utilize this mode of operation.

In the all-digital mode, two audio streams are fed from the same audio source. One robust stream provides the basic audio quality, but both streams are needed to provide the full quality. Thus, at the edge of the service area, the system can drop back from full to basic quality, avoiding the annoying cliff effect.

Carriers and Channels for IBOC

For hybrid IBOC, the digital service is achieved by placing additional carriers in the sideband areas above and below the analog signal of the associated AM or FM station. These carriers are arranged in a special way so as to minimize the interference to the analog portion of the signal. The digital signals fall within the existing emissions masks of the AM or FM channel as described in the previous chapter. In the all-digital mode, the analog audio service is removed and replaced with additional digital carriers.

The multiple carriers of COFDM used in IBOC are frequently referred to as *subcarriers*, and many people use the terms interchangeably. Strictly speaking, they are not really subcarriers, because they are not modulated onto another carrier, as is done, for example, with FM stereo signals or NTSC chrominance signals.

Modulation and Forward Error Correction

IBOC uses a special type of carrier arrangement called *coded orthogonal frequency division multiplexing* (COFDM) to carry the digital signal (see the Modulation section in Chapter 4 for a brief description of COFDM). Its main advantage for IBOC is that, when used in conjunction with techniques such as *interleaving* and *forward error correction* (FEC), COFDM makes the signal very robust and easier to receive under difficult conditions, particularly in a moving vehicle.

Audio Compression

Both AM and FM IBOC rely on audio compression to reduce the data rate of the digital audio to a size that can be carried in the available bandwidth. The audio codec (coder-decoder system) used for IBOC is known as HDC.

Typical uncompressed stereo audio at the IBOC standard sampling frequency of 44.1 kHz (as used for CDs) has a data rate of about 1.4 Mbps (megabits per second). This has to be reduced to no more than 96 kbps (kilobits per second) for FM IBOC and 36 kbps for AM IBOC.

HDC is based on the same *psychoacoustic* principles as the AC-3 system used for digital television; these are described in Chapter 15. It is outside the scope of this book to go into details, but, like most audio compression systems, HDC allows certain parts of the audio signal to be discarded, or sent with less accuracy, without significantly changing the sound heard by the listener.

AM IBOC

Sidebands and Bandwidth

The RF channel arrangement for AM hybrid IBOC is shown in Figure 13.1. The analog audio sidebands, carrying the mono analog program, extend to about 5 kHz on each side of the carrier, and the *digital sidebands*, carrying the digital service, extend out to just under 15 kHz. Although the term "digital sideband" is frequently used, they are not really sidebands in the traditional sense; they are actually just the areas of spectrum above and below the analog host where the digital carriers are placed. The primary, secondary, and tertiary "sidebands" carry different parts of the digital signal. As shown by the FCC AM Mask line, the digital carriers are at a much lower level than the analog signal, which helps reduce levels of interference into the analog host signal as well as into adjacent AM channels (see also Figure 12.1 in Chapter 12).

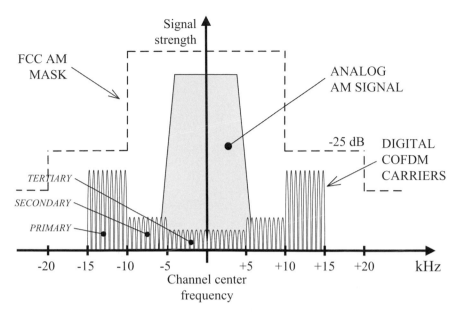

Figure 13.1. Hybrid AM IBOC RF Channel

In AM IBOC, the digital carriers are modulated using QAM (see Chapter 4). Using this technique, these carriers can also overlap the part of the channel used for the analog program service, as shown in the figure.

Nighttime Operations

The AM MF band in the United States is very congested with many stations. Because of the way AM MF signals are propagated over long distances after sunset, nighttime operation for AM stations is limited by interference from, and into, distant stations. At the time of the FCC's interim authorization of IBOC, no technical information was available about how AM IBOC would perform at night in the more difficult *skywave* propagation environment (see Chapter 17 for information on skywave propagation).

Following further consideration of these issues, including limited field trials, test measurements, and extensive computer simulations conducted by iBiquity, in March 2004 the National Association of

Broadcasters (NAB) made a recommendation to the FCC to extend the interim authorizations for AM IBOC services to nighttime use. While acknowledging the possibility for some interference into the fringe coverage areas of more distant stations, this recommendation concluded that the benefits to be gained for AM broadcasters and listeners far outweigh the limited interference predicted by the studies. If this recommendation is implemented, it will permit nighttime IBOC operations for all AM stations already authorized for nighttime analog broadcasts. The NAB has also asked for unexpected cases of interference to be dealt with by the FCC as they arise.

Quality and Bit Rates

Due to the presence of the digital carriers, when using IBOC the AM analog audio signal bandwidth has to be limited to approximately 5 kHz. Although analog AM stations can theoretically carry audio up to about 10 kHz, in fact most AM receivers cut off at frequencies below 5 kHz, so most listeners are not likely to notice this reduction in analog bandwidth. AM IBOC is not compatible with analog AM stereo; therefore, any AM stations still broadcasting in stereo will need to revert to mono for their analog service if they intend to broadcast IBOC.

The AM IBOC digital signal provides stereo audio at a quality comparable to existing FM radio, using audio compressed at 36 kbps. As a listener gets farther away from the IBOC transmitter, the AM IBOC digital audio signal blends from 36 kbps stereo to a 20 kbps mono signal that is carried as a more robust signal.

FM IBOC

Sidebands and Bandwidth

The RF channel arrangement for FM hybrid IBOC is shown in Figure 13.2. The analog audio sidebands extend to just under 130 kHz on each side of the carrier, and the "digital sidebands" extend out to just under 200 kHz. As shown by the FCC FM Mask line, the digital carriers are at a much lower level than the analog signal, which helps minimize interference into the analog "host" as well as the adjacent channels.

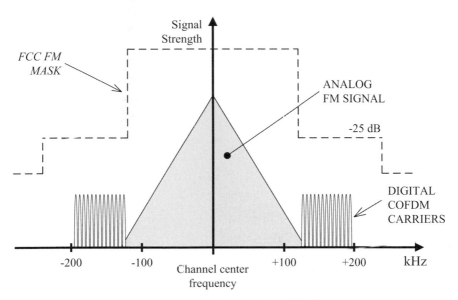

Figure 13.2. Hybrid FM IBOC RF Channel

Quality and Bit Rates

Unlike AM IBOC, no new restrictions are placed on the FM analog stereo signal when using IBOC. There is, however, an optional mode of operation for FM IBOC called *extended hybrid* in which the areas used for digital carriers are enlarged (toward the channel center frequency, and overlapping the analog signal area), allowing the IBOC signal to support additional data services. Although this mode not been evaluated by the NRSC, the extended hybrid mode is expected to have a minor impact on the quality of the host analog FM signal.

The FM IBOC digital *main program service* (MPS) provides stereo audio at near-CD quality, using audio compressed at 96 kbps.

Supplemental Audio Channel

It is possible to subdivide the 96 kbps digital signal into two or more audio streams, say at 64 kbps and 32 kbps, to provide a *supplementary audio channel* (SAC). The quality for the two channels can still be very good, and this gives stations the opportunity to broadcast different programs simultaneously. As compression technology continues to improve, this capability may enable stations to provide even more programming options.

IBOC Surround Sound

Demonstrations have been given of surround sound audio for IBOC, using special techniques for audio coding within the regular bandwidth available. In June 2004, SRS Labs, Inc. and iBiquity Digital Corporation announced the completion of joint testing of SRS Circle Surround® technology as a compatible surround sound format for HD Radio. Implementation of Circle Surround encoding allows radio stations to encode any content up to 6.1 channels into two-channel output for broadcast over the HD Radio system. This can be decoded at the receiver into full-bandwidth surround sound.

Digital Radio Data Broadcasting

Data Services Using Hybrid IBOC

One of the advantages that digital radio has over analog radio is an inherent ability to transmit data services along with the main channel audio signal. Both the AM and FM hybrid IBOC services support *program-associated data* (PAD) services, which allow for the transmission of station identification, song titles and artist names, and other program-related information; they can also accommodate other text such as weather and traffic updates. PAD information requires about 2 kbps of bit rate and can be displayed as scrolling text on a receiver's display panel. This is similar to the information available from an RDS subcarrier (used with analog FM radio broadcasts).

For FM hybrid IBOC, it is also possible to reallocate some of the bits normally used for the main channel audio signal to support transmission of additional audio channels or auxiliary data services. Another feature of the FM hybrid IBOC system, referred to as *extended hybrid*, can add 50 kbps of data capacity. AM IBOC, however, is essentially restricted to transmission of the main channel audio and PAD signals due to the relatively low 36 kbps capacity of the digital carriers.

Data Services Using All-Digital IBOC

The all-digital mode of IBOC provides much more space for new data services. In the future, IBOC stations will be able to transmit user-specific or locality-based messaging (e.g., for traffic, advertisements, and more sophisticated data services). Bit rates up to about 300 kbps for FM and 4 kbps for AM are expected, depending on the data rates allocated to the audio.

CHAPTER 14

NTSC Analog Television

As with radio, the FCC regulates all television broadcast transmissions in the United States. It stipulates what standards or systems must be used and licenses stations to operate on particular frequency allocations at specific power levels. As before, some international treaties also apply.

The arrangements for NTSC transmission were defined in the original NTSC specifications in 1941 and 1953, most of which are incorporated into the FCC rules. The FCC rules also specify various parameters, such as channels to be used, and the bandwidth of the transmitted signal. These rules enable U.S. stations to coexist with each other and allow receivers to operate in an optimum fashion. NTSC television signals use a combination of AM and FM modulation, with subcarriers for certain parts of the signal. In Chapter 12, we learned about these methods for radio transmission. If you understand the concepts discussed there, understanding analog TV transmission is quite straightforward.

Carriers and Channels for Analog TV

TV channels 2 to 13 are assigned in the frequency range 54 to 216 MHz in the VHF band. TV channels 14 to 69 are assigned in the range 470 to 806 MHz in the UHF band. However, not all frequencies in these ranges are assigned to television; there are some gaps for other services (e.g., the 88 to 108 MHz FM radio band) and for other purposes such as radio astronomy. In addition, changes in the FCC rules, related to spectrum recovery following the transition to DTV, mean that channels 52 to 69 will no longer be available for either analog or digital television broadcasting.

Each television channel in the United States is 6 MHz wide. The *visual carrier* (also known as the video or picture carrier) frequency is 1.25 MHz above the lower boundary of the channel, and the *aural carrier* (also known as the audio or sound carrier) center frequency is 4.5 MHz higher than the visual carrier. The color subcarrier is placed at 3.58 MHz above the visual carrier—all as shown in Figure 14.1.

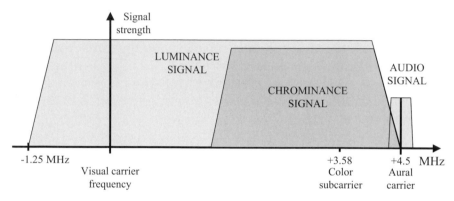

Figure 14.1. NTSC RF Channel

Sidebands and Bandwidth

In order to conserve radio spectrum, a form of AM modulation, known as *vestigial sideband*, is used for the visual signal. This means that most of the lower sideband of the TV visual signal is cut off, as shown in the figure. As explained in Chapter 4, the normal *double sideband* signal would extend from the video carrier minus the modulating frequency to the video carrier plus the modulating frequency.

Video Signal

Video Carrier

The video signal is amplitude modulated onto the video carrier. The process is similar to an AM radio station—except, of course, that the TV station is transmitting video information that is used by a TV receiver to paint a picture on the screen, whereas the AM radio station is transmitting audio information. In addition, the modulated AM picture signal occupies nearly 300 times as much of the radio frequency spectrum as a modulated AM radio signal. Although the lower video sideband is curtailed, the signal carries enough information to allow the receiver to recover the video picture; the demodulation process is slightly more complex than it would be with two full sidebands available.

Color Subcarrier

In Chapter 5, we explained how the NTSC chrominance information is carried on a subcarrier within the video signal. The way this works is similar to the subcarriers for stereo and ancillary audio services described in Chapter 12, with three main differences. The first is that this color coding is usually carried out early on in an analog system chain (e.g., at the studio camera), in order to allow single-wire video distribution. Also, to allow the two color difference signals to be carried, the color subcarrier is modulated using QAM (*quadrature amplitude modulation*). The third difference is that the subcarrier frequency is within the frequency range of the video luminance information. Although the receiver does its best to separate out the luminance and chrominance, there can be some interference of one with the other, called *cross-color*. This is why pictures with fine patterns, such as a check or striped jacket, can at times produce shimmering colored interference over the pattern. In that case, the particular brightness or luminance frequencies are being interpreted by the receiver as false color information.

Just as a mono radio ignores the stereo subcarrier and uses only the main mono program information, a black-and-white television ignores the color subcarrier and uses only the luminance information to produce the monochrome picture.

The reason that chrominance and luminance share some of the same frequencies is that, when color television was first introduced, the color subcarrier had to be placed within the existing video bandwidth so that the existing channel frequency allocations could be maintained. Otherwise, all stations would have needed new carrier frequencies, and existing receivers would have been made obsolete.

Audio Signal

The audio signal is frequency modulated onto the audio carrier at the top end of the television channel, as shown in Figure 14.1. The audio baseband signal may be a single mono audio channel or may include subcarriers for stereo and additional services, as discussed below.

Audio Subcarriers

As previously mentioned, the composite baseband signal of an analog television station's audio channel looks very much like that of an FM station, but with the stereo pilot frequency at 15.734 kHz instead of 19 kHz. In addition to the stereo signal, two standardized subcarrier channels are defined that can be carried with the TV audio signal: the separate audio program (SAP) channel and the professional (PRO) channel. The SAP channel is a mono audio channel that television broadcasters can use to transmit any type of audio information (it is often used for a second language track). The PRO channel is a narrower channel than the SAP channel, and therefore only permits voice transmissions or data information. The PRO channel, like the SAP channel, is optional, and not used by all broadcasters, but it is often used for communications with station staff at remote locations (e.g., for news gathering). An illustration of the typical analog TV station's aural baseband signal is provided in Figure 14.2.

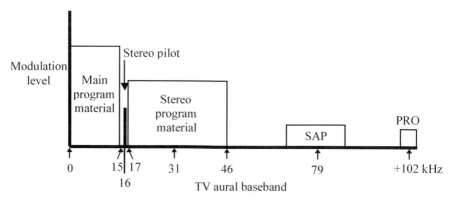

Figure 14.2. TV Aural Baseband Signal

Vertical Blanking Interval Ancillary Information

Because there is no picture information on the VBI lines (see Chapter 5), some of them can be used to carry additional, nonvideo information. The FCC has specified what type of information can be transmitted on various VBI lines. A summary is as follows:

Lines 1 to 9   *Vertical synchronization information only*
   (needed to ensure that the TV receiver knows this is the start of a new field)

Lines 10 to 18   *Test, cue, and control signals telecommunications (or other applications with prior FCC approval)*
   (e.g., control signals could be sent from a network to local affiliates to alert the affiliates to the fact that a local commercial break is coming)

Line 19   *Ghost canceling reference signal only*
   (planned to be used by receivers to reduce "ghosts" caused by signal reflections, but very rarely used)

Line 20   *Test, cue, and control signals; telecommunications (or other applications with prior FCC approval)*
   (see above)

Line 21   *Closed captioning and other program-related information only*
   (descriptive text used by hearing-impaired persons, "V-chip" content advisory ratings, and so forth)

Closed Captioning and Content Advisory Ratings

The FCC rules require broadcasters in the United States to carry closed captioning information for a certain percentage of most types of programming. This allows receivers to decode and display captions on screen, so hearing-impaired viewers can follow and understand the program dialogue and narration. Captioning text is coded into digital form at the studio and carried as a low-bit rate data signal inserted onto VBI line 21 in the video signal. This data is then modulated onto the visual carrier along with the rest of the video signal.

Line 21 can also carry other data associated with the program, in particular the *content advisory* information. This so-called V-chip rating can be displayed on screen and allows parents to control what types of television programs can be viewed by children. The system for closed captioning and other information carried in line 21 is specified in the Consumer Electronics Association (CEA) standard CEA-608.

Analog TV Data Broadcasting

VBI Data

It is possible to carry a limited amount of data in an analog television signal using spare capacity in the VBI, in a similar way that closed captioning is carried in line 21. About 12 kbps of data can be carried on each VBI line, and several lines can be combined to provide greater bandwidth. Several such services have been implemented at different times. In the United Kingdom and elsewhere, this includes a *Teletext* service that provides many pages of text and simple graphics pages, as well as program captions or subtitles. In the United States, analog datacasting has mainly been implemented in closed systems such as cable television, where the data decoder and user controls can be provided in the cable set-top box and remote control, although the Public Broadcasting Service (PBS) has also used the technique for various data services.

dNTSC In-Band Wideband Data

Recent developments have been made that allow an analog television station to transmit wideband data signals transmitted in the same channel as regular NTSC program material. Known as dNTSC (presumably for data NTSC), this allows data services to be carried that are similar to those proposed for DTV datacasting (see Chapter 15). The system, developed by Dotcast Inc., uses special techniques to reduce interference from the data signals into the television picture and sound to imperceptible levels. In this way, data services with bandwidth up to about 4.5 Mbps can be carried. Special receivers are required for this system, which is incompatible with other data broadcast systems.

In 2004, the Walt Disney Company introduced its MovieBeam® subscription service that uses Dotcast technology, over PBS member station channels. MovieBeam provides downloading of feature films as data files, which are then stored on a hard drive in the receiver set-top box, and can be played back on a regular television.

CHAPTER 15
ATSC Digital Television

ATSC stands for the Advanced Television Systems Committee, which developed the standards for DTV used in the United States (as well as in Canada, Mexico, and Korea). The principal standards comprise ATSC documents A/53 for digital television and A/52 for AC-3 audio compression. These standards were adopted (with the exception of the video formats table) by the FCC in 1996. Other standards for different aspects of the system have since been developed. In September 2004, the FCC adopted updates to A/52 and A/53, along with A/65B, the Program and System Information Protocol Standard (PSIP). As discussed in this chapter, DTV transmission is very different from analog TV, both in the type of video and audio signals and in the way they are modulated onto the RF carrier.

ATSC DTV signals are not compatible with NTSC. In order to receive the DTV transmissions, a new type of receiver is needed—either an integrated television or a set-top box. It is possible to use a DTV set-top box to feed an existing NTSC television, but to take advantage of the improved video quality, especially high definition and widescreen images, a separate HD monitor is required.

One fundamental difference between digital ATSC and analog NTSC television is that NTSC transmits complete pictures, but the ATSC system effectively sends the pictures broken down into many small parts, with a set of instructions to put them back together again. So, what is produced and seen in the studio may or may not be exactly what all receivers produce, depending on how they interpret the instructions. This is explained later in the section on video compression.

Carriers and Channels for DTV

Each NTSC station has been assigned a new channel for its ATSC DTV service. DTV RF channels are in the same VHF and UHF bands as NTSC television, using channels that were vacant in the FCC NTSC channel allocation plan. There were more vacant channels in the UHF band, so most DTV stations are in the UHF band. Changes in the FCC rules, related to spectrum recovery following the transition to DTV, mean that channels 52 to 69 will not have any digital television broadcasting at the end of the transition. In addition, some stations may move to a new DTV channel when analog broadcasting finally comes to an end.

As with NTSC, each DTV channel in the United States is 6 MHz wide. There is one carrier for each channel. A reduced-level carrier frequency, known as the *pilot*, is placed at the lower edge of the channel; the receiver needs this pilot carrier to help lock onto the incoming signal. Figure 15.1 shows a plot of the spectrum of an actual DTV transmission.

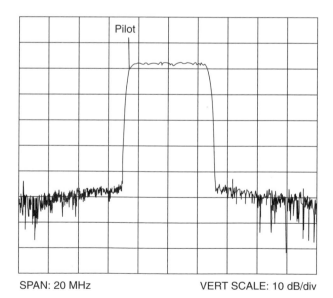

SPAN: 20 MHz   VERT SCALE: 10 dB/div

Figure 15.1. ATSC RF Channel

Channel Navigation and Branding

To make it easy for consumers to transition to the new digital channel for their favorite broadcast stations, the ATSC standard has a feature that uses the existing NTSC channel number as the *major channel* number for the DTV service, combined with a second *minor channel* number. The DTV major channel number helps the station retain its brand image. It can remain constant, even if the station has to move its DTV RF channel during the transition period. See the section on PSIP for more details.

Sidebands and Bandwidth

For reasons that are outside the scope of this book, the eight-level *vestigial sideband* (8-VSB) modulation used inherently produces numerous sidebands above and below the carrier frequency. To keep within the 6 MHz channel width, the upper sidebands are greatly reduced, and virtually all of the lower sidebands are cut off, leaving only a vestige of a sideband, as shown in the figure. Nevertheless, the reduced signal carries enough information to allow the data payload to be fully recovered by the receiver.

8-VSB Modulation

Digital Modulation

Eight-VSB is a special form of AM modulation using a single carrier modulated to eight different amplitude levels. The carrier is modulated with a *compressed bitstream* signal that, as explained later, carries all the information needed for the channel. This modulation occurs at the transmitter in a piece of equipment called an *exciter* (see Chapter 16 for more on exciters). The compressed bitstream input to the DTV exciter is processed and converted into digital *symbols*. The output of the exciter is a series of pulses of carrier wave, each with one of eight different amplitude levels that are assigned to eight symbols. These symbols are output at a rate of 10.76 million every second.

Transmitted Bit Rate

Each symbol is able to carry three bits of digital data. Therefore, the 10.76 million symbol per second output of a DTV exciter can represent $10.76 \times 3 = 32.28\,\text{Mbps}$ (megabits per second) of digital data. It is important to understand that the "data" being transmitted may represent video, audio, or other types of ancillary data information. Once in the bitstream, it is all referred to as data.

As explained in the later sections on compression and transport streams, the information bit rate for an ATSC bitstream is 19.39 Mbps. So why is the data rate coming out of a DTV exciter so much higher than the actual data rate of the video, audio, and ancillary information being broadcast? The additional bits are needed for forward error correction.

Forward Error Correction

Forward error correction (FEC) is used to make the signal more robust and able to withstand distortions in the transmission path. Multipath distortion is a common problem with over-the-air television signals, caused when multiple signals from the same transmitter arrive at the receiver at slightly different times (see Chapter 17 for more on information on multipath). There may also be various forms of interference such as lightning strikes that create large RF noise pulses, which can affect reception at great distances from the strike. Smaller RF pulses are created by electric motors, car ignition systems, and many other things. All of these conditions can cause data to be lost. The special error correction codes added to the DTV signal helps receivers to fix problems with the received signal. In addition, DTV receivers have special circuitry called *adaptive equalizers to* help cancel out the effects of unwanted signals.

Cliff Effect

With analog television, the received picture can be excellent (in areas of strong signal reception), mediocre, exhibiting "ghosting" and "snow" (in areas of marginal reception), or unwatchable (in areas of poor reception). ATSC DTV pictures never display ghosts because, so long as the receiver can decode the digital data that describes the picture, it can reconstruct a nearly perfect picture. However, under extreme conditions, with low received signal strength and/or strong multipath interference echoes, the DTV receiver may no longer be able to correctly decode the picture (and/or the sound). In that case, the picture and/or sound disappear completely. They go from perfect to nothing, with almost no intermediate stage. This is known as the "cliff effect," which is common to many digital transmission technologies.

ATSC Compressed Bitstream

The ATSC compressed bitstream, comprising digital video, digital audio, and ancillary data, is known as a *transport stream*. This is created by the *ATSC encoders* and *multiplexer* (see Figure 9.11 in Chapter 9), and delivered to the television station's transmitter at a rate of 19.39 Mbps. The transport stream is made up of blocks of compressed digital data, known as *packets*, which carry video, audio, and ancillary data. This is in contrast to the continuous stream of analog information for an NTSC signal.

The ATSC packets contain 188 bytes of data, but the first byte of each packet is used for synchronization, and an additional three packets are used for management of the bitstream, so 184 bytes are actually available for audio, video, data, and PSIP (see Figure 15.2).

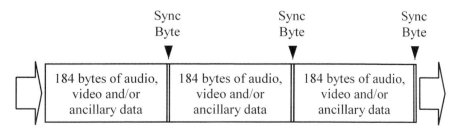

Figure 15.2. ATSC Data Stream

For comparison with the 19.39 Mbps data rate of the ATSC bitstream, the fastest broadband cable Internet connection available for the home can download data at about 5 Mbps, whereas a dial-up 56 kbps modem for a personal computer has a data rate of only 0.056 Mbps.

ATSC Video Formats

Most of the characteristics of digital video signals used for ATSC transmission are discussed in Chapter 6. The signal that is actually routed around the television studio and used for editing, recording, and so on can be one of various video formats—and in fact, some stations will likely continue to use their NTSC equipment in the studio throughout the early stages of digital television implementation. In order to broadcast an ATSC DTV signal, the station must have an ATSC encoder that is capable of encoding the signal format used by the station's studio equipment.

The video formats specified in the ATSC standard are listed in Table 15.1.

Table 15.1. ATSC Video Formats

Resolution Pixels × Lines	Aspect Ratio	Frame Rate Progressive or Interlace			
1920 × 1080	16 : 9	24P	30P	30I	
1280 × 720	16 : 9	24P	30P		60P
704 × 480	16 : 9	24P	30P	30I	60P
704 × 480	4 : 3	24P	30P	30I	60P
640 × 480	4 : 3	24P	30P	30I	60P

There are 18 different formats listed. This becomes 36 if the same formats using the small frame rate adjustment mentioned in Chapter 6 are counted. The number of pixels and lines refer to those displayed in the actual picture. Horizontal and vertical blanking intervals are not transmitted in DTV, hence the VBI lines used for closed captioning, and so on in NTSC cannot be used.

You may note that the numbers of lines and pixels for the 480-line formats are slightly different from those listed as standard definition video production formats (720 × 483) in Chapter 6. The small number of extra lines and pixels have to be discarded so the picture can be broken down into the right size pieces for compression.

There is no 1920 × 1080 format at 60P (60 progressive frames per second), because the high data rate needed to transmit this format cannot be transmitted within the limited amount of bandwidth (6 MHz) available for television broadcasting in the United States. In the future, this may be achieved using more efficient compression systems than currently specified. The 1280 × 720 format does not include a 30I version (30 interlaced frames per second), because there is no existing 720-line interlaced video format with which compatibility has to be maintained.

The 704 × 480 interlaced 4:3 format is used to transmit programs produced as standard definition digital video, or for existing NTSC video signals converted to digital. The 640 × 480 formats were included for compatibility with the computer VGA graphics standard, but are rarely, if ever, used for DTV.

The table of video formats shown above was the one part of the ATSC DTV standard on which all parts of the industry could not agree. Hence, when the FCC incorporated the standard into its rules, the video format table was omitted completely. Broadcasters are therefore allowed to transmit any available video format. In reality, most broadcasters use the 1080-line 30I or 720-line 60P formats for high definition, and 480-line 30I for standard definition. The 24P (film rate) formats will likely see increasing use in the future because they occupy less bandwidth than other formats of the same resolution.

Video Bit Rates

As shown in Chapter 6, the total bit rate for uncompressed HD video is 1.485 Gbps, and for SD video 270 Mbps. These rates are far higher than the payload that can be transmitted in the 19.39 Mbps

ATSC bitstream; therefore, it is necessary to first reduce the rate using *compression*.

MPEG-2 Compression

The ATSC standard is based on using *MPEG-2* video compression. MPEG is the Moving Pictures Experts Group, an international standards-setting organization that has developed several standards for compressing digital video. Compression is an extremely important aspect of the ATSC system—without it, transmitting digital television would not be practical. So, what is compression?

Put simply, to compress digital video means to discard unneeded parts of the signal and encode the remaining parts in a manner that reduces the total amount of data required to store or transmit the video. All this needs to be done without noticeably degrading the picture quality. The process is performed by a powerful computer known as an MPEG-2 or *ATSC encoder* using a computer program called a *compression algorithm*. The output of the encoder is a bitstream containing packets of compressed video data. The DTV receiver has a complementary *decoder*, to re-create the picture quality, and the coder/decoder system is known as a *codec*.

The compression algorithm used for ATSC video is complex and outside the scope of this book to explain properly. We will, however, briefly discuss some of the basic principles in order to provide a general understanding of the process.

Discard Unneeded Data

The first basic principle is the elimination of all information that is not actually needed to produce the picture. Some of the data that can be discarded is the signal that occurs during the horizontal and vertical blanking periods, where there is no picture. In addition, the amount of picture color detail can be reduced without being noticeable to the human eye. In Chapter 6, we discussed chrominance subsampling; this process is done to a greater degree in video compression. In some cases, the amount of luminance (brightness) detail may also be reduced.

Exploit Redundancy

Video frames often have a great deal of redundant information that can be reduced or eliminated to decrease the amount of data that needs to be sent. A shot of a still picture is an extreme example. Instead of transmitting a stream of identical pictures 30 times per second, the DTV system could send just one complete frame of information, and then an instruction to the receiver to repeat the frame over and over, until it changes.

Even within a single frame, there may be redundancy. For example, let's assume that a particular video image has a red horizontal line one pixel high and 100 pixels in length extending across the screen. The uncompressed video data for this image might include instructions such as the following:

> Display pixel 1 in red
> Display pixel 2 in red
> Display pixel 3 in red
> . . .
> Display pixel 99 in red
> Display pixel 100 in red

However, the compressed video data for this image could include instructions such as these:

> Display pixel in red
> Repeat 99 times

thus greatly reducing the amount of data while effectively sending the same information. This type of coding within a frame is called *intraframe* coding.

Motion Estimation and Interframe Coding

Television pictures often have an object that does not change much from frame to frame, but just moves across the screen. Often, it is possible to predict where it is heading in the next frame by looking at where it came from in the previous one; this is called *motion estimation*, and it provides part of the picture information that is transmitted. In addition, MPEG-2 limits the encoded information for some frames and sends only what has changed since the last picture. Exploiting the redundancy of information between different frames is called *interframe* coding and further reduces the amount of new information that needs to be sent to construct the next frame.

MPEG Frames

When displayed on a television receiver or monitor, ATSC video signals, like NTSC video signals, produce a rapid-fire series of still pictures, known as *frames*. In NTSC video, each frame is, from a technical viewpoint, identical all the way from camera to television receiver. That is, although the picture data carried changes from frame to frame, the type of frame remains constant. However, the makeup of ATSC video frames as they are transmitted is different from how they are produced in the studio and how they are displayed at the receiver. There are three distinct frame types produced by MPEG-2 compression: *intracoded* frames, *predictive coded* frames, and *bidirectionally predictive coded* frames. These are generally referred to as I-frames, P-frames, and B-frames.

Figure 15.3. I-Frame

An I-frame is *intracoded*, using compression techniques only within its own borders. Thus an I-frame is a complete picture and can be

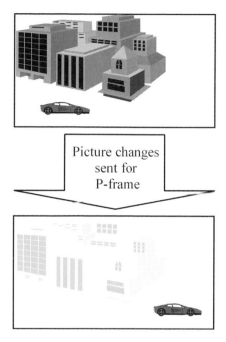

Figure 15.4. I-Frame Followed by P-Frame

decoded and displayed at a receiver by looking only at the data within itself.

A transmitted P-frame contains only the "change" information needed to re-create a video frame in conjunction with the previous I-frame that is already at the receiver. In further detail, at the decoder, the motion estimation information that accompanies a P-frame is first applied to the previous I-frame to generate a predicted frame, and then the P-frame is added to yield a complete video frame.

A transmitted B-frame contains the very small amount of "change" information needed to re-create a video frame when combined with information from two other frames, a previous I-frame or P-frame and a subsequent I-frame or P-frame. Like a P-frame, a B-frame cannot stand by itself.

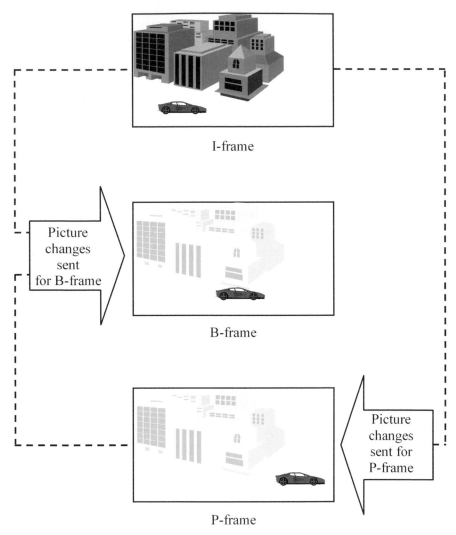

I-frame

Picture changes sent for B-frame

B-frame

Picture changes sent for P-frame

P-frame

Figure 15.5. B-Frame Between an I-Frame and a P-Frame

The transmitted P- and B-frames always carry less new information than an I-frame, and therefore help reduce the data rate
needed. The number and order of P- and B-frames between two I-
frames is called a *group of pictures* (GOP) and may vary for different MPEG encoders. Long GOPs have many P- and B-frames and
thus reduce the data rate best. The disadvantage of long GOPs,
however, is that the extended time between I-frames slows down

picture acquisition when channel surfing, and the GOP is also more susceptible to interference.

Buffering

It may seem counterintuitive that a particular frame in a video stream could be reconstructed, in part, from a future frame that has not even made it to the screen. How this happens is that the digital ATSC video stream does not arrive at a television set and immediately get displayed on the screen. During the decoding process, the video data is temporarily stored, processed, and then forwarded to the screen. The "store and forward" process is called *buffering*, a common practice in digital transmission. While the video data is temporarily stored in the receiver, the computer circuitry in the decoder has an opportunity to process or manipulate it. A similar buffer is used at the MPEG encoder so that the order in which the frames are transmitted can be changed for the particular GOP sequence being used.

As noted earlier, a B-frame is constructed with information from both previous and subsequent frames. For the receiver to be able to construct a B-frame, the two frames from which it is predicted must be transmitted before the B-frame. For example, if three frames of video have been encoded at the studio with an I-frame first, a B-frame second, and finally a P-frame, the order will be changed using the buffer in the encoder. The I-frame will then be transmitted first, followed by the P-frame and then the B-frame. The receiver can then receive and store the information for both the I-frame and the P-frame before it has to decode the B-frame.

This is a good place to point out that the buffering needed for this process is the primary reason a brief delay occurs between the instant the viewer selects a new DTV program and when the new program appears on the screen. Also contributing to this delay is the fact that, in order to begin decoding the new video stream, the decoder must wait for the next I-frame to be transmitted for that program. This is because the I-frame is the only one that can stand by itself without any previous frames to use for prediction, so in order to begin decoding a new stream of video, a receiver must start with an I-frame.

Efficient Encoding

Finally, after removing the redundant information, the data that is left to send can be coded efficiently, taking advantage of the variations in the makeup of the video pixel information. An example of efficient coding is Morse code, which uses combinations of dots and dashes to transmit text messages letter by letter. The letter E typically occurs most often in the English language, so that is coded as a single dot symbol. However, an infrequently used letter, such as Q, is coded with four symbols (dash, dash, dot, dash). Thus, a typical message would be sent with more short codes and less long codes, reducing the amount of data required.

Although the type of compression used in ATSC video is much more sophisticated than described here, one can see how it is possible to code raw video data in a manner that requires less data overall to transmit but does not significantly degrade the picture. MPEG-2 is capable of reducing raw video bit rates by a factor of 60 or more.

Decoding

As described previously, during the compression process, portions of the original video stream are discarded, and the remaining portions are encoded in a manner that reduces the total amount of data to be transmitted. Although this signal that is transmitted over the air contains enough information to re-create a video image on the television screen, it does not directly carry all of the video data for each pixel of every picture. Instead, it effectively carries the instructions that enable the computer circuits inside a DTV receiver to re-create the image. The DTV receiver therefore decodes and decompresses the video data, and then reconstructs the frames of video before sending them to the display device.

Advanced Compression Systems

Recent developments in compression technology allow high-quality encoding with much greater efficiency than MPEG-2. In particular, the AVC/H.264 system (developed in conjunction with MPEG) and the VC-1 system (based on Microsoft Windows Media 9) provide equivalent picture quality at about half the bit rate or less. Such systems allow more programs to be transmitted in less bandwidth. However, because of the necessity not to make existing DTV receivers obsolete overnight, broadcasters must continue to use the MPEG-2 standard for many years to come. Various proposals are under consideration to allow the new, more efficient codecs to be used in some circumstances.

AC-3 Audio

The digital audio that accompanies ATSC video has a very different format from that used in NTSC television or traditional radio broadcasting. In particular, it has the capability for surround sound with 5.1 channels, and it is compressed to reduce its data rate for transmission.

As discussed earlier, in NTSC the video signal and the audio signal are transmitted on two separate carriers. ATSC transmission has a single signal that is a continuous stream of data packets. Each individual data packet can carry audio, video, and/or ancillary data. It is up to the ATSC receiver to sort them all out.

The packets of audio data in an ATSC signal conform to a system developed by Dolby Laboratories called AC-3 (for Audio Coding–3), which is also known as *Dolby Digital*. The specifications for this system are part of the ATSC standard. The system offers many improvements over NTSC audio. One of these is that noise and interference are virtually eliminated; another important feature is that it enables *surround sound* to be carried.

Surround Sound

AC-3 is designed to provide up to six channels of surround sound. One of these is a *low frequency effects* (LFE) channel that provides low-frequency audio to a subwoofer speaker that enhances audio effects, such as explosions or trains passing by. Because of the limited audio frequency range carried over the LFE channel, this channel requires much less data to convey its audio information than the other, "normal" audio channels. For this reason, the LFE channel is sometimes considered to be only one-tenth of a channel, and the overall ATSC audio system is known as a 5.1 (rather than 6) channel system.

The six channels of audio are intended to be heard through speakers that are generally positioned as shown in Figure 15.6. Because very low frequency sounds are nondirectional, the position of the low-frequency subwoofer is not critical, so this speaker can usually be positioned wherever it is most convenient.

When surround sound is not needed for a program, AC-3 can also carry regular two-channel stereo or single-channel mono signals.

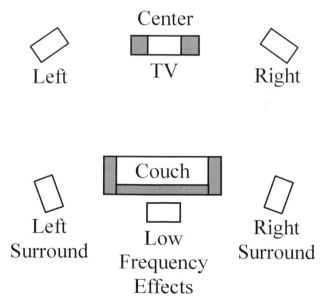

Figure 15.6. Layout of Surround Sound Speakers

Additional Audio Services

In addition to the main program audio in the principal language, the ATSC system allows for one or more additional versions of the audio track to be carried with alternative languages that can be selected at the receiver.

AC-3 is also designed to allow other services to be carried simultaneously, to be selected by the viewer to supplement or replace the complete main service. These are as follows:

- Service for the visually impaired
- Service for the hearing impaired
- Associated service—dialogue
- Associated service—commentary
- Associated service—voice-over
- Main service—music and effects
- Emergency information

The *Visually Impaired* service is an audio channel used to describe the video scene that it accompanies. Its purpose is to allow visually impaired people to "watch" a television program by receiving periodic audio updates of the on-screen activity.

The *Hearing Impaired* service is an audio channel that contains dialogue that may be processed for improved intelligibility by hearing-impaired viewers. (Closed captioning information, which can also be provided for hearing-impaired viewers, is transmitted separately as video data.)

The *Dialogue, Commentary, and Voice-over* services were designed to be used when required with a *Music and Effects* service, which contains only the music and effects from the program and not any dialogue. This was intended as an alternative method to enable multiple language versions of the same program to be broadcast. Using this method, a viewer theoretically can receive the video and accompanying music and effects, and then select between the different languages available from the Dialogue, Commentary, or

Voice-over services. Because of the complexity involved in creating several separate dialogue signals to accompany the same music and effects, this combination is not currently used. In any case, few, if any, DTV receivers have the two AC-3 decoders that are needed to implement this feature.

The *Emergency (E)* service permits the insertion of emergency messages into the audio stream. Whenever an emergency message is present, an ATSC receiver should stop playing other audio and play the emergency message. Once the emergency message has finished, the other audio will resume.

Audio Compression

If uncompressed digital 5.1 surround sound were transmitted, it would take up more than 4 Mbps of the 19.39 available bitstream data rate. The most important feature of the AC-3 system is that it allows high-quality compression of the audio signals, reducing its data rate by a factor of about 12.

AC-3, like most audio compression systems, is a *perceptual coding* system that relies on human *psychoacoustic* principles to allow certain parts of the audio signal to be discarded, or sent with less accuracy, without significantly changing the sound heard by the listener. Some of these principles include the following:

- Sounds are inaudible if they are below a certain level, which varies with frequency.
- Loud tones mask soft tones of a similar frequency occurring at the same time. In most cases, the human hearing system will not even recognize the existence of the quiet tone.
- Louder sounds mask softer sounds immediately after or before the occurrence of the louder sound. Again, they will not be heard.

Therefore, the digital bits used to represent the sounds that would not be heard anyway can be discarded without perceptibly altering the audio. After bits have been discarded, special digital coding techniques can be used to further reduce the bit rate. It is beyond the scope of this book to discuss how this is done, but one general example will give you the general idea.

Let's say that the numerical values associated with individual digital sample points in a segment of audio are:

5, 12, 7, 9, 5, 12, 7, 9, 5, 12, 7, 9, 5, 12, 7, 9, 5, 12, 7, 9

This could be represented by simply transmitting each individual value. It is also possible, however, to transmit "5, 12, 7, 9" followed by the instruction "repeat four more times." In this way, the amount of data necessary to transmit a long series of repetitious values can be reduced.

An AC-3 encoder uses these techniques, and other acoustical and mathematical attributes, in a sophisticated way to code raw audio data in order to reduce the data bit rate, while not significantly degrading the sound that is heard. The output of the encoder is a bitstream containing packets of compressed audio data.

Other Compression Systems

Although AC-3 is widely used for DTV, it is by no means the only compression system for audio encoding. Several other systems are widely used in radio and elsewhere. These include an earlier Dolby system called AC-2, also MPEG-1 layer 1, MPEG-1/2 layer 3 (usually known as MP3), and the more recent MPEG AAC (*Advanced Audio Coding*). The recent systems provide much higher audio quality at lower bit rates. There are continuing developments, and a technique called *Spectral Band Replication* (SBR) further improves high-frequency audio response in low-bit-rate applications.

Multiplexing

As previously mentioned, the compressed bitstream fed to the transmitter is known as a *transport stream* and contains video, audio, and ancillary data packets. The compressed video packets

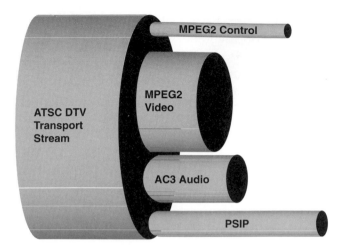

Figure 15.7. Data Pipe Concept of the ATSC Transport Stream

from the MPEG encoder and the compressed audio packets from the AC-3 encoder for a particular program are combined or *multiplexed* together to produce the transport stream. At the same time, other system information data such as *PSIP* (see later section) is added to the multiplex, together with ancillary data (if any) for *datacasting* (see later section). Figure 15.7 illustrates how the ATSC transport stream can be considered as a large data "pipe," which is divided up into smaller "pipes" carrying multiple types of information. Don't forget that in reality all of this information is being sent as serial data (i.e., as bits sent one after the other down a single channel).

Quality and Bit Rates

Video Quality

There are various considerations for video quality, including the following:

- *Spatial resolution* (sharpness or crispness of the picture)
- *Temporal resolution* (how well motion is portrayed)

- *Video noise* (unwanted "grain" or "snow" or other interference on the screen)
- *Brightness, contrast,* and *color accuracy*
- *Compression artifacts* (various)

The spatial and temporal resolution of the picture is largely determined by the video format selected (number of lines, pixels, and frame rate). With DTV, there should be little, if any, degradation in these parameters caused by the transmission system. It's the same for video noise, and distortions in brightness, contrast, and color—the picture is either perfect or not there at all.

Compression Artifacts

If insufficient bits are used to encode the video, the resulting picture exhibits degradations known as *compression artifacts*. The most noticeable are *pixelation* and *blocking*. When this happens, instead of natural-looking pictures, the picture breaks up instantaneously into small or larger rectangles with hard edges, either in particular areas or all over the screen. This may happen continuously or just at particular difficult events such as a dissolve, when every video pixel is changing.

No specific formula can be used to calculate exactly how many bits per second are needed to transmit a given program at a certain quality level. The data rate needed is not a constant number. It is partly dependent on the frame rate and the resolution, but it also depends very much on the subject matter of the picture. All else being equal, higher resolution, higher frame rates, and video with lots of detail and motion in it all require higher data rates.

Using MPEG-2 compression, HD video can be satisfactorily encoded at rates between about 12 and 19 Mbps, and SD video at rates from about 2 to 5 Mbps, depending on picture content. For material originally shot at 24 frames per second (film rate), the bit rate can be reduced by about 20 percent compared to 30-frame interlaced material, with similar quality.

Audio Quality

There are various considerations for audio quality, including the following:

- *Frequency response* (how well high and low tones are reproduced)
- *Distortion* (harsh or rough-sounding audio)
- *Audio Noise* (unwanted "hiss" or "static")
- *Dynamic range* (how well loud and soft sounds are reproduced)
- *Compression artifacts* (various)

The frequency response, distortion, noise levels, and dynamic range of the audio are largely determined by the audio coding system used and how well it is set up. With DTV, little, if any, degradation in these parameters should be caused by the transmission system. The audio is either perfect or not there at all.

Audio compression artifacts are not usually noticeable with a well-set-up system and are rarely objectionable. However, if too few bits are used, there may be a "swishy" or "watery" sound in the upper midrange and high-frequency areas. Another possibility is a "gritty" quality to the audio, which can sometimes be attributed to too much audio resolution being taken away in an effort to use fewer bits.

AC-3 bit rates needed for encoding audio are well established for each audio format. Typically, 5.1 audio is allocated 384 kbps, and stereo 192 kbps, although other rates can be used.

Multicasting

The total bit rate for a program service comprises the audio and video bit rates plus a small amount for system information. In many cases, a single DTV program may require less than the 19.39 Mbps available for transmission. When this occurs, it is possible to transmit multiple program services over the same DTV channel. This is done by adding additional video and audio compressed bitstreams to the multiplex and is known as *multicasting*.

Typically, broadcasters wanting to maintain the highest video quality do not exceed one HD program or four SD programs in the multiplex at one time. However, it is quite common to have one HD and one SD program together, or more SD channels if they include mainly static pictures, such as graphics or weather radar. Some stations may change their program mix at different times of the day, perhaps broadcasting four SD programs during the day, and switching to one HD and one SD program in the evening.

It is important that the total data rate for all of the program streams added together does not exceed the total data rate available in the DTV channel. For example, a single DTV channel might be capable of carrying four different programs most of the time. However, if these programs contain commercials that have a lot of motion and scene changes in them, the single DTV channel may not be able to handle a commercial on every single program at the same time.

Statistical Multiplexing

An important technique that can be used to help maintain the highest video quality while multicasting is called *statistical multiplexing*. This takes advantage of the fact that on average (i.e., statistically), different programs have different amounts of picture detail and motion at any one time. The multiplexer varies the bit rate allocated to each program on demand, to allow each one the bit rate it needs to maintain high quality. It will be rare for all programs to require maximum bits at the same time, which could result in *bit starvation*, causing compression artifacts.

Closed Captions

In NTSC, the information needed for carrying closed captions for the hearing impaired is carried as data on line 21 in the vertical blanking interval. The VBI lines are not encoded with MPEG compression, so in ATSC the captioning data is carried in another way. Within the video compression system, space is reserved in an area called the *video user bits* for carrying this additional data.

The DTV closed captioning system is specified in the Consumer Electronics Association (CEA) standard CEA-708. When this system was designed, the opportunity was taken to enhance the capabilities compared to NTSC captions. Thus, DTV captions can have a choice of fonts in different colors and sizes and at different locations on the screen, several caption services can be provided simultaneously (e.g., adding captions for different languages or for "easy reading") and there are other enhancements.

Program and System Information Protocol (PSIP)

We have learned that ATSC DTV carries one or more program services using a digital bitstream carried in a single television RF channel. The FCC rules require broadcasters to carry *Program and System Information Protocol* information, usually known as PSIP, in accordance with ATSC standard A/65. This is transmitted in the multiplex with the DTV program bitstream. PSIP helps the viewer navigate to the correct program, provides an electronic program guide for current and future programs, and helps the DTV receiver tune to the correct channel and correctly decode the program.

PSIP is carried as a series of data tables that are regularly updated and carried in the DTV "pipe," as shown conceptually in Figure 15.7 earlier in the chapter.

Major and Minor Channels

NTSC television stations in the United States have assigned call letters but typically brand themselves in a particular market using their broadcast channel number. The digital station is known by the same call letters, but with the suffix "DT" for digital television. It is, however, transmitted on a new TV channel with which viewers may not be familiar. PSIP allows the digital services to be identified with a number that relates to the well-known NTSC channel number.

PSIP includes a *Virtual Channel Table* (VCT) that, for terrestrial broadcasting, defines each DTV service with a two-part number consisting of a *major channel* followed by a *minor channel*. The major channel number is usually the same as the NTSC channel for the station, and the minor channels have numbers depending on how many DTV services are present in the DTV multiplex, usually starting at 1. Different arrangements, with one-part numbers, are used for ATSC services carried on cable channels. The VCT also includes the name given to each service. A station might label one service as their call letters with the suffix "HD" and, if they are multicasting, another might be labeled as SD, or some other name.

As an example, at the time of this writing, the analog channel 9 station, WUSA-TV, in Washington, D.C., identifies its two over-the-air digital services as follows:

Channel 9-1   WUSA-DT
Channel 9-2   9-Radar

Minor channel number 0, if used, must indicate the NTSC program service for the station (the NTSC programs are not actually in the DTV bitstream, but they may be listed in the program guide). Services consisting only of data, with no video or audio, must use minor channel number 100 or greater.

Electronic Program Guide (EPG)

PSIP includes *Event Information Tables* (EITs) that provide a program schedule for each DTV program service, which allows the receiver to build and display an electronic program guide (EPG). The EITs should carry information for at least the next 9 to 12 hours of programs, and may include information up to a maximum of 16 days ahead. As well as the basic data for each program of title and start time, the information should include *content advisory* rating, audio format (e.g., stereo, 5.1), language, and closed caption details.

Extended Text Tables (ETTs) may carry additional descriptive information about each program that may be displayed.

Directed Channel Change

Directed Channel Change (DCC) is an interesting feature that allows
broadcasters to tailor programming or advertising based on viewer
demographics. For example, viewers who enter location information, such as their zip code, into a DCC-equipped receiver could
receive commercials that provide specific information about retail
stores in their neighborhood. Segments of newscasts, such as
weather alerts that are relevant to certain areas, could also be targeted based on this location information. A channel change may
also be based on the program rating or the subject matter of the
content of the program. Nearly 140 categories of subject matter
have been defined that can be assigned to describe the content of
a program. A broadcaster can use this category of DCC request
switching to direct a viewer to a program based on the viewer's
desire to receive content of that subject matter.

DTV Data Broadcasting

As previously stated, the transmission system for digital television
can be thought of conceptually as a large pipe for carrying the
digital bitstream, which is divided up into smaller pipes for different program services. We have also learned that video and audio
program material for DTV is carried as digital data—a series of bits
of information. All computer systems and networks, including the
Internet, use bits to process, store, and carry different types of
information, whether it is a text document, a numerical spreadsheet, graphics, audio, or moving pictures. It is perhaps not surprising that, in addition to regular television programs, the DTV
pipe can be used to carry these other types of digital information.

Several different standards exist for the different types of *data broadcasting* (also known as *datacasting*), both in the United States and

elsewhere; details are beyond the scope of this book. It is worth noting that efforts have been made in the United States to achieve harmonization between the broadcast and cable industry in this area, and the resulting standard for broadcasting is known as the Advanced Common Application Platform (ACAP). Other data services may be carried, however, that do not comply with ACAP.

Bandwidth

The ATSC DTV pipe carries a total of about 19.39 Mbps of data, which is known as the *bandwidth* of the channel. As discussed previously, the amount of space needed for television video and audio depends on the number and type of programs carried. It is possible that there may be spare bandwidth, not needed for video and audio programs, and this may vary considerably at different times of day or even from instant to instant, depending on picture content.

A particular television station decides how much of its bandwidth to allocate to data broadcast services; this may be a fixed amount ranging from a few kilobits per second to several megabits per second, comparable to a high-speed broadband Internet connection.

Opportunistic Data

Even if no fixed bandwidth is allocated for datacasting, there will always be some spare bits available in the bitstream due to the variations in picture content in the television programs. These spare bits can be used for *opportunistic data* services that are delivered at an indeterminate data rate. This data is transmitted whenever an opportunity becomes available in the ATSC signal. For example, even if a high definition program is being transmitted, there will be times during the program when the data rate necessary to carry the video information will be reduced, such as when a still picture is on the screen. At that point, more capacity is available for data services.

Data Piping, Data Streaming, and Data Carousel

Depending on the type of datacasting service, the data required may be sent as a "package delivery" (e.g., downloading a file) or as "streaming" for continuous data delivery.

In some cases, the data may be sent repeatedly in a *data carousel*, which provides more opportunities for downloading the data to the receiver.

Types of Data Services

There are two basic types of datacasting service: those that are associated with a regular television program, known as *program-related data*, and those that stand-alone, *nonprogram-related data*. Examples of program-related services include the following:

- Supplementary information related to the program
- Sports statistics and additional game or player information
- Opinion polls or voting as part of a show
- Home shopping for products featured in a show

Some DTV receivers may be designed to display the additional program-related data services, inserted over the program pictures, with picture-in-picture techniques, or with separate screens, all selectable on the remote control.

Examples of nonprogram-related services include the following:

- News, weather, stock quotes
- Web pages
- Newspaper/magazine download
- Music/movies download
- Software download

Some DTV receivers may be designed to display the additional nonprogram-related data services in some manner, selectable on the remote control. However, in some cases, the data may be intended for use on a computer or some other device and will not run directly on a television.

Interactive Services

Interactive implies that the viewer interacts with the data service, sending messages to request more information or services, or to provide feedback. This may require the use of a *back-channel* (also known as a *return-channel*) that sends the viewer's request back to the source of the service at the broadcast station or elsewhere. Digital cable television systems have the capability for a back-channel from the home built into the system, because the cable can transport information in both directions. However, since broadcasting is one-way only, over-the-air broadcasters have to provide an alternative path for the return signals. This typically uses a dial-up telephone line, although communication over the Internet is another possibility; other arrangements, using radio transmission, have been proposed.

Examples of true interactive services include quiz or game show participation, polling, or home shopping services, and any service that requires additional information to be sent from the source of the data service upon request from the viewer. However, some services that appear to be interactive do not actually require a back-channel. In that case, what happens is that all of the data that relates to a particular feature (e.g., supplementary program information) is downloaded automatically to the receiver and is already there when the viewer presses the button to display it or search for information, so the request does not need to be sent back to the source.

Conditional Access

Data services may be provided free of charge or for a fee. *Conditional access* systems allow broadcasters to charge for a particular service, either on a subscription basis or on a pay-per-use basis. Arrangements for this are similar to those used by cable and satellite companies for premium TV channels and pay-per-view and usually require a *smart card* to be used for access, with charges billed to a credit card account.

Data Broadcast Receivers

Some DTV receivers and set-top boxes are designed to display the additional program-related data services. Typically, these have additional buttons on the remote control to control and request the additional information, and the receiver has memory to store at least some of the data that is received. Other types of data services are intended to be used on a computer. Computers can have a DTV tuner added to receive such services or, in some cases, it may be possible to connect a computer to a DTV set-top box. With the convergence of technologies, the line between television and computer devices is becoming blurred, and we already have television receivers with hard disk storage. Increasingly, all such devices will have network capabilities, allowing the possibility of sharing digital media.

CHAPTER 16
Transmitter Site Facilities

For many reasons, including antenna coverage, zoning, and space requirements, the best location for the transmitting antenna for a radio or television station is often different from the preferred location for the studio facilities, where convenience of access and other considerations may be more important. In that case, the transmitter and antenna will usually be located at a separate site, with the program feed provided by a studio-transmitter link. On occasions, it may be possible for the transmitter equipment and antenna to share the same site as the studios, in which case the studios and transmitter facilities are said to be *co-sited*.

Viewed overall, transmitter sites for all types of broadcast facilities (AM, FM, and TV, analog and digital) have some similarities. As a rule, most transmitter sites will have at least the following categories of equipment, all as shown in Figure 16.1:

- Studio-transmitter link (STL) (see Chapter 11)
- Processing equipment to prepare the signal for transmission
- Transmitter *exciter* to create the low-power version of the RF signal to be transmitted (except for AM stations)
- Transmitter *power amplifier*(s) to produce the high-powered signal for broadcast
- *Transmission line* to carry the signal from the transmitter to the antenna
- Transmitting *antenna* (with AM, the tower itself is the antenna)
- *Tower* to support the antenna

The exciter and power amplifier together are usually referred to as the *transmitter*.

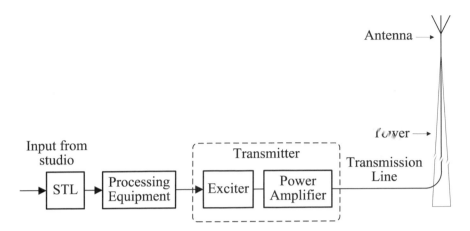

Figure 16.1. Transmitter Site Block Diagram

Although all AM, FM, and TV transmission facilities have a lot in common, the details vary greatly—even more so for digital IBOC and DTV equipment. There are also major differences in the types of antennas that are used. Let's first talk about the arrival of the signals at the transmitter site.

Incoming Feeds

All signals, whether they are audio or video, analog or digital, arrive at the transmitter site via the studio-transmitter link (STL) (see Chapter 11). Both analog and digital STLs are still used for radio and television stations, except that for DTV the STL has to be digital. If the particular audio and/or video signals coming out of the STL are not what is required to feed the transmitter processing equipment or the exciter, they are fed to analog-to-digital or digital-to-analog converters before going to the next links in the chain.

Audio signals out of the STL are typically stereo left and right channels for FM, IBOC, and TV stations, or there may be a mono feed for an analog AM station. Some FM and NTSC TV stations may send composite stereo audio on the STL from the studio, ready to feed direct to the exciter.

Video signals from the STL for an analog TV station are usually composite analog NTSC, but they may be sent from the studio as component digital video that then has to be converted to analog for transmission. DTV signals almost always arrive at the transmitter site in the form of a single digital bitstream, ready to feed direct to the exciter.

Processing Equipment

AM Audio

AM stations are now usually mono only; the audio processor needed to optimize the sound of the station may be located at the studio or at the transmitter site. If the station is also transmitting IBOC, and a common STL is used for the audio, it has to be at the transmitter site.

FM and NTSC Audio

Both for analog FM radio and analog TV stations, the *stereo generator* is used to create the composite stereo signal, as described in Chapter 12. The stereo generator has two main inputs—left and right channel audio. It has a single composite baseband output comprising the mono, stereo, and pilot signals, as shown in Figure 12.3 on page 210.

For stations carrying ancillary audio services, the SCA subcarrier is combined into the composite audio signal, as shown in Figure 12.4, either in the stereo generator or in a separate SCA device. Radio data system (RDS) information, if provided, is also added here.

Some stations place the stereo generator at the studio and feed the composite signal over the STL. Others feed component left and right audio and ancillary audio over the STL and place the stereo generator at the transmitter site. The second arrangement has to be used if a radio station is transmitting IBOC and analog services with a common STL.

Typically, the output of the stereo generator is fed into the exciter (see later section) for modulation onto the station's main carrier. Sometimes the audio processing equipment to make the station's audio sound louder and clearer is installed before or after the stereo generator; several different arrangements are possible.

IBOC Audio

Separate left and right audio signals must be sent to the transmitter site for both AM IBOC and FM IBOC stereo transmissions. If this is sent over a separate STL from the analog service, then audio processing to optimize the sound of the station may be carried out at the studio or before feeding into the IBOC encoder at the transmitter site. However, the degree of processing for the analog service is different than for IBOC, so if a common STL is used, then the separate processing for IBOC and analog must be at the transmitter site.

NTSC Video

If the video signal arrives at the site on an analog STL, it will be in a composite video form ready to feed direct to the NTSC video exciter with little, if any, processing required. If it arrives as component digital video, it needs first to be converted to analog composite video.

DTV Bitstream

The DTV compressed bitstream sent to the transmitter contains the complete and final video and audio program signals. No further processing needs to be done at the transmitter before feeding to the exciter.

Exciters

The *exciter* is the device that takes the baseband audio, video, or digital bitstream baseband signal and converts it to a radio frequency signal with the appropriate method of modulation. The output of the exciter is at a low level and has to be amplified further to produce the high power needed to feed the antenna. Sometimes the exciter is installed inside the transmitter housing, but otherwise it is a separate unit installed in an equipment rack next to the transmitter.

AM Radio

Most analog AM radio transmitters (except for those transmitting stereo) do not have an exciter. Instead, the amplitude modulation process takes place in the power amplifier, as described later.

FM Radio

For FM radio, the exciter takes the incoming composite audio signal and frequency modulates it onto an RF signal at the station's carrier frequency.

AM IBOC

The AM IBOC exciter takes audio inputs for both the analog and digital services. It modulates the IBOC service onto the digital carriers using QAM and COFDM and amplitude modulates the analog signal onto the station's main carrier. The combined composite output is then fed to a single common power amplifier.

In the exciter, the analog audio is delayed by several seconds to ensure that the analog and digital audio is in sync at the output of the receiver. This is necessary because the digital signal path intrinsically has several seconds of delay (typically between 6 and 8 seconds). Some of the delay is caused by digital signal processing and some by the *diversity delay* buffer. Diversity delay provides extra robustness in reception of the signal by mitigating problems due to short interference events (e.g., temporary signal loss that can occur with a moving vehicle).

FM IBOC

FM IBOC stations may utilize separate exciters for the analog and digital portions of the signal, but they typically use a single combined exciter unit. The combined exciter takes audio inputs for both the analog and digital services. It modulates the IBOC service onto the digital carriers using COFDM. If the station is using a common transmitter/power amplifier for IBOC and FM services, it also frequency modulates the analog signal onto the station's main carrier, after applying the diversity delay as for AM IBOC. The combined composite output is then fed to a single common power amplifier.

For stations that install a new IBOC transmitter, while retaining their old FM transmitter, the delayed analog audio is fed out of the IBOC exciter and connected to the input of the existing analog FM exciter. In that case, the IBOC exciter composite output feeds only the IBOC power amplifier.

NTSC TV

In analog television, there are two exciters: one for video and one for audio. The video exciter takes the incoming composite video signal and amplitude modulates it onto the station's video carrier. The aural exciter takes the incoming audio signal and frequency modulates it onto the station's aural carrier. These two signals may feed one or two power amplifiers (see later section).

ATSC DTV

In digital television, a single exciter takes the digital ATSC data stream and modulates it onto the station's carrier, using the 8-VSB version of amplitude modulation.

Power Amplifiers

The second main part of a broadcast transmitter is the *power amplifier*. This takes the modulated input from the exciter and amplifies it to the high-power radio frequency signal needed to drive the antenna (for traditional analog AM transmitters, the arrangements are somewhat different—see later discussion). Power amplifiers for analog and digital transmission generally use similar components, although the way they are set up and used may be very different. It may be possible to convert some (but not all) of the newer models of transmitters from analog to digital operations. Transmitter power output (TPO) may vary from as small as a few hundred watts (W, the unit of electrical power) to many tens or even hundreds of kilowatts. An example of a high-power UHF television transmitter is shown in Figure 16.2.

Figure 16.2. UHF Digital Television Transmitter
Courtesy of Lawson & Associates, DesignTech, and KDTV

Tubes and Solid-State Devices

The heart of many power amplifiers is one or more high-power electron tubes. There are various different types of tube, which work best for particular wavebands and output powers. The most common transmitting tube devices are *tetrodes*, *klystrons*, and *inductive output tubes* (IOTs), but there are others. How these work is beyond the scope of this book.

For various reasons, all electron tubes wear out. They typically have to be replaced every few years, although this varies greatly for different transmitter and tube types. To get away from the tube-replacement routine, many modern transmitters have been designed using all-solid-state electronics. Solid-state power amplifiers use the same principles as transistors and integrated circuits and are very reliable. Although they do not require periodic tube replacement, some of the high-power amplification components can still fail and require replacement, but typically not for many years.

Although they are much more reliable, solid-state electronics are not usually used for the highest-powered transmitters, such as those used in many UHF TV stations, because they are considerably less efficient than tubes and, at high powers, would produce excessive electric power costs.

Cooling Systems

The tube or solid-state components in a power amplifier get very hot during operation and must be cooled. This is done either with cold air being blown through the transmitter, or with a liquid cooling system something like that used for cooling the engine on a car—using a radiator outside the building to dump the heat.

AM Radio

Traditional analog AM broadcast transmitters are fundamentally different from most others. In this case, the RF input to the power amplifier is typically an unmodulated carrier wave from a device called an *oscillator*. After first being amplified, the incoming program audio signal is also fed to the power amplifier; the amplitude modulation process for the carrier then takes place in the power amplifier.

AM IBOC

Because AM IBOC requires the analog and digital signals to be modulated together, they have to share a common power amplifier. It may be possible to upgrade some newer analog transmitters for this purpose, but frequently a new transmitter is required.

FM IBOC

FM IBOC has four alternative transmission arrangements: low-level combining, mid-level combining, high-level combining, and dual-antenna. In low-level combining, the analog and digital signals are combined together in the exciter and then share a common power amplifier. In high-level combining, they have separate power amplifiers, and the outputs are combined in a *diplexer* (see later section). Mid-level combining is a combination of the low- and high-power combining techniques and may be advantageous for stations with moderate (in the order of 10 kW) power outputs. The dual-antenna system has two completely separate power amplifiers and antenna systems, one for the analog portion of the IBOC signal and one for the digital.

NTSC TV

In the most common configuration for a VHF analog television station, the video and audio exciters feed their output signals into two separate power amplifiers. Then, the outputs from the two power amplifiers are combined and fed up a single transmission line to the antenna. However, most UHF transmitters mix the audio and video signals together within the transmitter, and they share a common final power amplifier stage. In both cases, the transmitted audio power is 10 percent of the video power.

ATSC DTV

DTV uses a single power amplifier. In some cases, it may be possible to convert newer models of analog TV transmitters to carry a digital signal.

Transmission Lines and Other Equipment

The *transmission line* (also known as a *feeder*) that connects the transmitter or diplexer to the antenna is usually a length of *flexible* or *semiflexible coaxial cable, rigid coaxial feeder*, or *waveguide*. A type called *open wire* feeder is occasionally used, mostly for shortwave stations.

Flexible or semiflexible coaxial transmission line is like an extremely thick piece of cable television wire. How thick depends on the amount of power it has to handle from the transmitter (too thin and it might overheat), and may range from about an inch to several inches in diameter. Rigid copper pipes are used to make the nonflexible type of coaxial feeder. These have a piece of pipe threaded through the center of a larger piece of pipe, kept exactly centered by installing plastic spacers between the inner and outer pipes. Rigid coaxial lines, as their name implies, cannot be bent, and special angle sections are needed to change direction. They can be used for very high power antenna feeds, with sizes up to about 12 inches in diameter—the size required depending on the signal power and frequency.

Waveguides are best described as "duct work for radio frequencies" and do not have a center conductor or any of the insulating material associated with it. In fact, they look much like the metal ducts you might find in an air-conditioning system. Without going into details, radio waves propagate down waveguides by reflecting off the inside of the metal walls of the guide. Waveguides are the most efficient type of broadcast transmission line; that is, more of the transmitter's energy makes it to the antenna without being lost as heat compared to other types of transmission lines. The main disadvantage of waveguide is that it is considerably larger than coaxial transmission line, and therefore it is more difficult for a broadcast tower structure to support. It is most often used with high-power UHF transmitters, where the short wavelengths keep the size manageable and its superior efficiency helps save a significant amount of electric power.

Dummy Loads, Diplexers, and Reject Loads

It is rare for a broadcast transmitter to be connected directly to the antenna with the transmission line. Usually, there is some sort of large switch or connection panel that allows the transmitter signal to be fed to a *dummy load* at the transmitter building. The dummy load accepts the RF power and turns it into heat, allowing the transmitter to be tested without transmitting over the air.

It is also common to have two or more transmitters feeding into one antenna for reasons that include the following:

- High-level combining of TV video and audio signals for one channel
- Combining FM IBOC and analog signals at high level
- Combining dual transmitters of any type for redundancy
- Combining multiple TV transmitters on different channels to share one antenna

In these cases, the two transmission lines from the transmitters will be connected to a diplexer that allows two signals to be combined together. There are also arrangements for multiple transmitters, in which case the device is called a *multiplexer*. Sometimes, in order to balance the system, it is necessary to feed a proportion of the signal to a *reject load* rather than the antenna; this load turns the unwanted signal into heat, as with a dummy load.

Whether or not transmitters can be combined to feed one antenna depends on many factors, largely related to the design of the antenna, but also on the transmitter channels and output power. Under some circumstances, combining the station's NTSC and DTV transmissions may be possible.

AM Antenna Systems

The antenna is one thing that differs greatly from one type of broadcast service to the next—AM, FM, or TV. The main reason is that, in order to operate efficiently, the length of any antenna (transmitting antenna or receive antenna) must be related to the *wavelength* of the transmitted signal. For efficient operations, generally the antenna will be somewhere between 1/4 wavelength and 1/2 wavelength long. As noted in Chapter 4, radio waves used for broadcasting have a wide range of wavelengths, ranging from one or two feet for UHF television waves to hundreds of feet for AM radio waves, so the antennas also vary greatly.

AM Antennas

The wavelength for AM transmissions is several hundred feet, depending on the frequency. Therefore, an AM radio station's transmitting antenna is usually simply the station's tower. The actual metal structure of the tower is *hot* (i.e., energized with electrical energy from the transmitter), and it can severely shock or kill a person who touches it while standing on the ground. For this reason, the FCC requires this type of tower to have a fence around it that will keep people away. The height of the tower depends on the transmitting frequency of the station and whether it is a 1/4-wave or 1/2-wave antenna. Generally, the lower the station's frequency, the taller the tower, with a range up to about 450 feet.

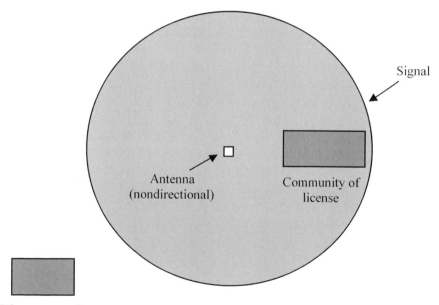

Figure 16.3. Nondirectional Horizontal Antenna Pattern

A single tower will have a nondirectional horizontal radiation pattern, transmitting the same amount of energy in all directions, as shown in Figure 16.3.

Directional Arrays

Sometimes, multiple AM radio towers are used together as part of a *directional antenna* (DA) system, called an *array*. An AM directional antenna array involves two or more tall radio towers standing in a straight line, or sometimes standing in a parallelogram formation. The purpose of the DA is to direct the transmitted energy toward the community of license and to reduce the energy traveling in directions where it might cause interference to other licensed stations. Generally speaking, the larger the number of elements in the array, the more directional the pattern. Figure 16.4 shows an example of a directional *horizontal radiation pattern*. A directional antenna is said to have a certain amount of *gain* in the direction of most power, when compared to a nondirectional antenna, and this increases the *effective radiated power* (ERP) of the station, which is frequently much larger than the transmitter power output (TPO).

In many instances, AM stations are authorized by the FCC to operate in a nondirectional mode during the day but are required

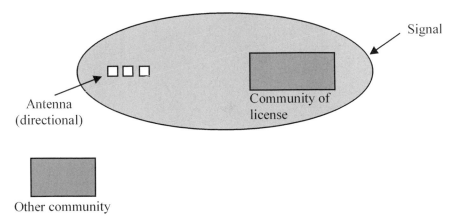

Figure 16.4. Example of Directional Horizontal Antenna Pattern

to use a directional mode at night. The reason for this is that an AM transmitter that does not interfere with signals in other communities during the day may do so at night as a result of *skywave* propagation. For more information about skywave propagation and the FCC's methods for preventing interference with other broadcast stations, see Chapter 17.

Ground Radials

Another important component is the antenna *ground radial* system. AM radio waves traveling across the surface of the earth (the *ground wave*, see Chapter 17) depend on *ground conductivity*. They need an excellent connection to the ground at the transmitter site to give the signal a good start as it leaves the transmitter. This is achieved with a series of ground radials, which are copper wires buried in the ground, extending outward from the base of the antenna for several hundred feet in a pattern, as shown in Figure 16.5. A standard AM ground radial system will have many more equally spaced radials than shown in the drawing (typically 120), and the actual length of each ground radial is a function of the transmitting frequency of the station. The lower the transmitting frequency, the longer the radial.

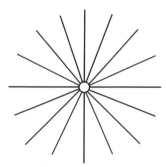

Figure 16.5. Overhead View of AM Ground Radials

Because of their dependence on ground conductivity, AM radio transmitting antennas are usually found near the communities they are intended to cover, at approximately the same ground level.

AM IBOC Antennas

Many antenna systems used for analog AM broadcasting should also be able to carry AM IBOC signals. In some cases, it may be necessary to adjust some parameters on the antenna and/or the transmission feed line to optimize performance of the system.

FM and TV Antennas

Wavelengths in the FM and TV wavebands range from just over a foot for the highest UHF TV frequencies to about 10 feet for FM radio. Although antenna designs do vary somewhat for FM and TV, the concepts are not very different, so we will cover them together.

FM and TV transmitting antennas are usually found near the communities they are intended to cover and are mounted as high as possible, usually on a tall tower. Where it is practical, the tower is located on the highest terrain in the area, often a mountain where available. This is because the short wavelengths of FM and TV band signals tend to travel in straight lines and do not "flow" around obstacles. They therefore perform best when there is an unobstructed path between the transmitter and receiver (i.e., line-of-sight). In addition, they are less dependent on ground conductivity for propagation than AM band waves are.

Also because of their short wavelength, FM and TV antennas are much smaller than AM antennas, typically ranging from somewhat less than a foot to about five feet long. They are electrically isolated from the tower on which they are mounted, which is grounded and consequently safe to touch. The antennas are sometimes made up of multiple *elements*, which affect the directional pattern.

The antenna elements are mounted on their supporting structure with clamps or other mounting hardware, and the complete antenna assembly is then attached to the supporting tower. The antenna is fed with the signal from the transmitter by the transmission line that extends from the transmitter up the tower to the antenna.

Multiple Bay Antennas

You may have heard FM or TV antennas referred to as "single bay," "2-bay," or "4-bay," and so on. The word *bay*, in this case, means a single antenna. Multiple bay antennas are often used in FM radio and TV transmission because they make the transmission system more efficient by changing the *vertical radiation pattern* to focus the beam and reduce the amount of energy sent up into the sky, and sometimes to reduce the amount of signal that is transmitted toward the area in the immediate vicinity of the tower, which would otherwise receive more signal than it needs. The more bays that are added to an antenna system, the more focused the transmitted signal becomes. For example, Figure 16.6 shows how the transmitted signal from a 2-bay antenna might differ from the transmitted pattern of an 8-bay antenna.

A multibay FM or TV antenna operates using the same principles as an AM directional antenna (DA). The major difference (aside from the frequency, and therefore the size of the antenna elements)

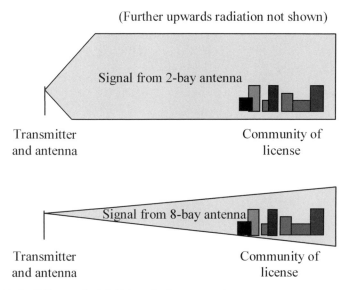

Figure 16.6. Effect of Additional Antenna Bays on Vertical Radiation Pattern

is that the multiple antennas in an FM or TV array are stacked vertically on the tower, whereas the multiple antennas in an AM DA are lined up horizontally along the ground. The result is that the FM or TV multibay antenna focuses its transmitted energy in the vertical direction, whereas the AM DA focuses its energy in the horizontal direction.

It should be noted that in some instances it is necessary to focus an FM or TV signal in a particular horizontal direction, as shown in Figure 16.4. Some antenna systems are designed for these purposes, using concepts similar to those described previously. Pattern adjustments can be made electronically by adjusting the *phase* (timing relationship) between the signals that arrive at each of the antennas in an antenna array. In this way, it is possible to create complex patterns to cover particular target areas while protecting other directions from unwanted signals.

FM IBOC Antennas

Most antenna systems used for analog FM broadcasting should be able to also carry the FM IBOC signals without significant adjustments. In the alternative dual-antenna arrangement for FM IBOC, the IBOC signal from the digital transmitter is fed to a separate second antenna, which must be in close proximity to the first. In that case, the analog transmitter and antenna system are left unchanged.

Combined Channel Antennas

It is possible to combine the outputs of two or more transmitters on different channels together and feed the combined signal up the tower to a single *wideband* antenna. This is most often done where tower space is at a premium (e.g., in large cities such as New York). It is also done elsewhere where there are good reasons to do so and can result in great savings in space and cost.

Most antennas operate most efficiently over a narrow range of frequencies, but special designs are available to handle multiple channels. The channels to be combined have to be within a certain range, because the wider the range of frequencies to be handled, the greater the compromises in antenna performance that have to be accepted.

ATSC DTV Antennas

Requirements for antennas for DTV are generally similar to those for NTSC transmissions. There may be different coverage and power considerations for the DTV service, which will be on a different channel from the station's NTSC service.

Towers

Towers are of two main types: *self-supporting towers* and *guyed towers* (also known as *masts*), which are held up with guy wires (sometimes a special type of nonmetallic rope) attached to anchors in the ground. Self-supporting towers are usually in the range up to about 1000 feet high, and guyed towers go up as high as about 2000 feet.

It is also common for broadcast antennas to be mounted on short structures on top of existing tall buildings, particularly in city locations with skyscrapers. This avoids the cost of a separate tall tower. Special provision has to be made to house the transmitter equipment in a suitable space within the building.

As previously mentioned, AM towers usually form the actual transmitting antenna. However, for all other bands, the tower is used to support the antenna, either fastened to the top of the tower (top-mounted) or to the side of the tower (side-mounted). Antennas may be open to the elements or protected inside a fiberglass radome. One tower frequently supports antennas for more than one transmitter, including FM radio, NTSC TV, and/or ATSC DTV. More than one station may often share the same tower, along with other, nonbroadcast services such as cellular telephony. In some cases, antennas for FM radio, cellular telephony, and so on can be mounted on an AM antenna (i.e., tower), which gives an AM antenna owner the opportunity to make additional revenue by leasing tower space.

Markings and Tower Lights

According to FCC and Federal Aviation Administration (FAA) regulations, towers over 200 feet high have to be painted in red and white stripes and/or fitted with lights to help indicate the location of the tower obstruction to aviation traffic.

Wind Loading and Icing

The tower has to be designed to safely withstand the strongest winds that occur at the site, taking account of all the extra loads imposed by the antennas and transmission lines. This is important to remember when changes or additions to antenna systems are planned (e.g., when adding a DTV antenna). Quite frequently, tower strengthening may be required.

Depending on the tower location, accumulations of ice on the tower and antennas in cold weather may be a major issue, affecting the design and construction of the tower. De-icing heaters are commonly installed in extreme climates.

Translators and Repeaters

As mentioned earlier, FM and TV radio signals tend to travel in a line-of-sight fashion and do not flow around obstacles. This means that in regions with uneven terrain, there may be population centers that, while within the intended service area of the station, are in a valley or behind a ridge and completely hidden from the view of the transmitter, and therefore unable to receive the service. To overcome this obstruction, an antenna and high-quality receiver are installed at a suitable high location that can receive the main station. The output of the receiver is converted (*translated*) directly to a new RF frequency (without converting it to baseband audio or video) and retransmitted with a directional antenna toward the area where it is needed. These *translators* typically operate at low powers between about 1 and 100 watts.

In some cases, the fill-in transmitter operates on the same frequency as the main transmitter and is then known as a *repeater*. Repeaters, again, are often low-power devices, but some stations may be licensed to operate high-power repeaters. Other stations use multiple translators and/or repeaters in a "daisy chain" arrangement to carry the signal onward to remote locations.

Transmitter Remote Control

The majority of broadcast transmitters in operation today are connected to a remote control unit. For many years, the most popular remote control systems have used two hardware devices, one located next to the transmitter and one at the remote control point, usually the associated studio on-air master control room. These devices are connected by a communications link, which may be a dial-up or dedicated phone line or a communications channel on the studio-transmitter link (STL). The units communicate with each other using techniques similar to how computers communicate over a phone line using modems.

The unit at the transmitter has a series of *control contacts* that are connected by extension cable to the switches that control the transmitter. It also has connections that monitor the status of the transmitter (e.g., on or off, alarms and fault conditions, various voltage and power readings). A complementary unit at the studio location has switches and indicators that automatically mimic those at the transmitter; they allow an operator to control and monitor the transmitter as though he or she was at the transmitter site.

The number of controls and indicators will vary greatly from system to system. In addition to interfacing to the transmitter, most remote control systems also include other connections for site functions, such as temperature, power, security alarms, and in particular, monitoring and switching of a directional antenna, and the state of the tower lights. Remote control systems are usually able to automatically print out the values of the various transmitter meter readings that are required to be recorded by the FCC. These become part of the station log.

Remote Dial-up

Some systems allow a transmitter engineer to call the remote control unit from any touchtone phone and control the switches in the remote control unit—and, by extension, the switches on the transmitter—by pressing buttons on the telephone. The transmitter may also report its status with messages over the phone.

Computer-Based Remote Control

Modern remote control systems have computer monitors and keyboards at the studio control point, which allow for a better human interface and increased capabilities. More sophisticated still are *network monitoring* systems, which often work over computer networks (including the Internet) and are able to provide complete management of transmitter sites and other facilities.

Modern transmitters usually have remote control connections like the serial port or network connection on a computer. These do not need the hardware switch contacts box and can connect directly to the communications link to the studio control point.

CHAPTER 17

Radio Wave Propagation and the FCC Rules

This chapter discusses aspects of the Federal Communications Commission's (FCC) rules that regulate broadcasting in the United States, and explains the propagation characteristics for the different broadcast frequency bands, which influence the rules for different types of stations.

FCC Rules

The FCC's technical rules have the primary objective of ensuring that a broadcast station's signal does not cause unacceptable amounts of interference to another broadcast station's signal or to signals in other telecommunications services.

Another objective of the FCC rules is to ensure that the signals transmitted by the nation's broadcasters are of good technical quality. These last objectives are met largely by requiring compliance with the various standards developed for the different types of broadcasting.

Frequency and Power Allocations

In order to ensure that stations do not interfere with one another, the FCC has adopted complex rules regarding the allocation of broadcast frequencies and power to each station. These rules are based on the propagation characteristics of the broadcast signals involved. Propagation characteristics are the particular qualities of a signal that determine how it behaves as it travels through the atmosphere (i.e., how far and in what direction).

The FCC rules and frequency allocation procedures require different broadcast signals on the same or adjacent channels to be geographically separated by appropriate distances. Different rules also require that each broadcaster's signal must stay in its allocated part of the radio spectrum. These are the FCC's emission masks and modulation limits, which help ensure that one station's signal does not bleed over into the channels of other stations located next to it on the dial.

AM radio stations have distinctly different propagation characteristics from FM and TV stations, and the FCC has therefore adopted somewhat different allocation procedures for AM stations than for FM and TV. The propagation characteristics of TV and FM signals are similar, so the FCC uses a substantially similar procedure for determining whether a proposed TV or FM channel can be allocated to a particular station.

These differences of propagation are important because they affect the coverage that is achieved from a particular site, the transmitter power that is needed, and the potential interference into other stations on the same or adjacent channels. As mentioned in Chapter 4, because of their different wavelengths, the carrier waves used for AM, FM, and TV transmissions have different properties for how they propagate through the air. Let's look at the main characteristics and also some of the considerations for digital transmissions.

AM Propagation

Skywave

What makes an AM signal so different from an FM or TV signal is the need to consider *skywave* propagation, which affects the MF band used for AM but not the VHF and UHF bands used for television. *Skywave* is a phenomenon that occurs after sunset when radio signals bounce off the *ionosphere* layer high in the Earth's atmosphere, as shown in Figure 17.1.

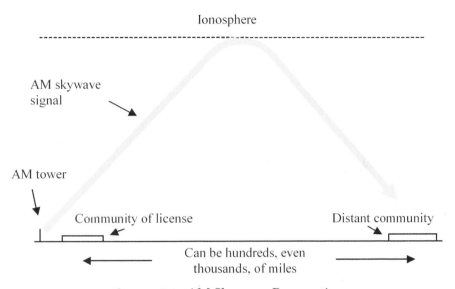

Figure 17.1. AM Skywave Propagation

As shown in the figure, an AM signal is capable of traveling from its transmitter to a distant city, while skipping over many places in between. For this reason, care must be taken when allocating an AM frequency to a new station to ensure that the transmissions at night will not cause unacceptable levels of interference because of skywave propagation to distant AM stations on the same or adjacent channels.

Because of the need to protect other AM stations from skywave propagation, the FCC allocates some AM frequencies to stations on a daytime-only basis. These stations are generally called *AM daytimers*. It is also common for AM broadcasters to be granted permission to operate at night, but at a much lower power.

During the daytime, skywave propagation is not an issue for AM transmissions, because a lower layer of the Earth's atmosphere, generated by the sun's rays only during the daytime, absorbs upward-bound MF band AM radio waves, and the long-distance propagation disappears.

Groundwave

FCC rules are also intended to protect broadcast stations from each other's *groundwave* signals. Although skywave propagation of AM signals occurs only at night, groundwave propagation is constant for both daytime and nighttime.

The groundwave signal, as the name implies, travels over the earth's surface at ground level. How far the groundwave signal travels, for a given transmitter power and antenna, is largely a function of the Earth's *ground conductivity* over the route being traveled by the signal. The higher the conductivity, the better the AM signal travels. *Ground conductivity* is a measure of the resistance of the ground to electrical signals, which varies considerably in different geographical regions, as shown in Figure 17.2, based on a map in section 73.190 of the FCC rules.

FM Propagation

There are basic differences between the way an AM groundwave and an FM signal propagate (e.g., FM VHF band radio waves do not propagate by skywave at night). The FCC's rules for allocation of FM radio channels are, therefore, very different from the rules for AM channels. In this case, neither skywave nor groundwave propagations are issues. The main considerations are line-of-sight and distance.

Line-of-Sight Propagation

Generally speaking, as radio frequencies get higher, they become increasingly dependent on having a line-of-sight view between the transmitter and the receiver. FM band signals tend to have this characteristic, and their propagation is generally not dependent on the conductivity of the ground they are traveling over.

To understand this point, think about visible light, which has wavelengths that are much shorter than broadcast radio waves. Light

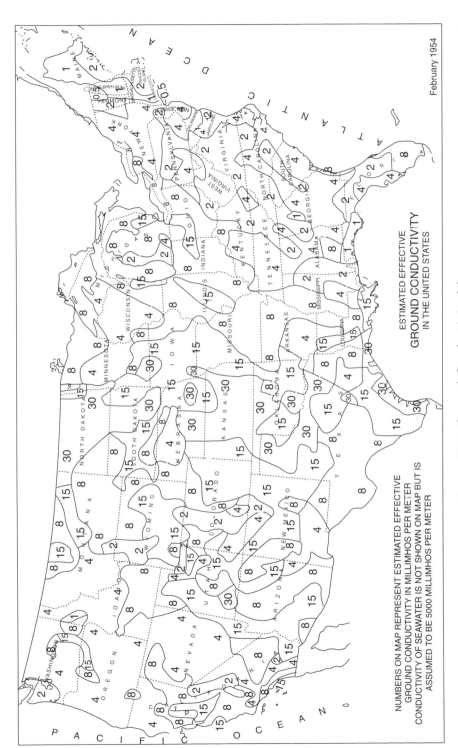

NUMBERS ON MAP REPRESENT ESTIMATED EFFECTIVE GROUND CONDUCTIVITY IN MILLIMHOS PER METER CONDUCTIVITY OF SEAWATER IS NOT SHOWN ON MAP BUT IS ASSUMED TO BE 5000 MILLIMHOS PER METER

ESTIMATED EFFECTIVE
GROUND CONDUCTIVITY
IN THE UNITED STATES

February 1954

Figure 17.2. Ground Conductivity Map

has a hard time getting around any obstruction and casts a hard shadow. However, AM waves, with wavelengths in the hundreds of feet, are able to follow the surface of the earth and largely "flow" around obstacles or even mountains. FM band waves, with shorter wavelengths than AM, come somewhere in between, but they perform best in an environment with no obstructions.

The FCC's frequency allocation procedure for FM radio stations takes into account factors including the general layout of the land around the proposed antenna site and the distance between the proposed site and other stations on the same and adjacent channels. For FM stations at the lower end of the FM band, the distance to the nearest TV channel 6 transmitter is also taken into account, because channel 6 is just below the edge of the FM band.

Multipath

Another characteristic of the shorter wavelength FM signals is their tendency to reflect off the earth's surface when they encounter an obstruction. They will also reflect off objects such as buildings and large vehicles such as airplanes and buses (much as light reflects of shiny surfaces). Therefore, an FM transmitter located in an area where there are mountains or large hills may have major propagation problems for two reasons. First, the signal from an FM transmitter located on one side of a mountain will have a hard time reaching the other side because the mountain will block the primary signal. Also, there may be reflections off one or more hillsides, producing some transmitted energy in a different direction from that in which it was originally traveling.

This results in a phenomenon called *multipath interference,* which, as the name implies, occurs when FM receivers get signals, from the same FM transmitter, via more than one path. An illustration of this concept is shown in Figure 17.3. Although the two received signals are similar, they will be slightly out of phase (i.e., one of them arrives at the receiver a small fraction of a second after the other). Because of this, it is often called an *echo.*

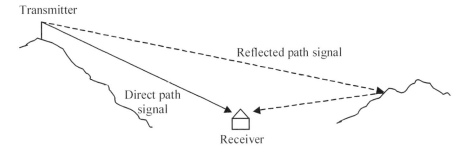

Transmitter

Figure 17.3. Illustration of Multipath Interference

The phase difference of the two signals causes them to interfere with one another. In another example, multipath manifests itself as the "picket fencing" effect that motorists may notice on their car radios as they move slowly in a city street. The picket fencing, or repetitive noise and distortion, is caused by two or more multipath signals bouncing off buildings near the street. As the car moves, the reflected signals alternately add and subtract from the main signal, which causes the interference.

IBOC Considerations

The system design for IBOC is intended to approximately replicate the primary service area of the analog channel with the digital program service. However, the system designers acknowledged that some people listen to the analog transmissions at greater distances and lower signal strengths, accepting the increased noise and distortion that may occur. The digital service is not usually receivable at all under these conditions. Furthermore, it was considered necessary for the digital service to degrade gracefully at the edge of the service area, and for the listener not to have to suffer the "cliff effect." Therefore, the system was provided with the capability to blend more-or-less seamlessly from the digital to the analog service at the receiver, depending on the reception conditions.

The IBOC system, using COFDM modulation, was specifically designed to resist multipath interference, which therefore does not normally cause IBOC reception to fail.

TV VHF and UHF Propagation

TV signals in the VHF and UHF bands propagate in basically the same manner as FM signals, but UHF signals are even more directional and dependent on line-of-sight transmission.

Multipath

Multipath interference, discussed earlier with regard to FM signals, can also cause distortion in the received audio signal from an NTSC TV station. Multipath will also cause the *ghosting* effect that many people will have seen at some time with their received analog TV video. Ghosting occurs when one or more video signals from the same NTSC transmitter arrive at the receiver at slightly different times. This causes additional images (ghosts) to be painted on the screen, which are displaced sideways because they are slightly delayed.

Antenna Height

An FM or TV signal is able to "see" further, and therefore propagate over longer distances, if its antenna is raised up higher. Therefore, if an antenna is raised to a new location from its originally authorized height, the FCC rules require the broadcaster to lower the station's authorized transmitter power. Conversely, if the antenna is moved to a lower location, then the transmitter power may be increased. Such an antenna rearrangement may occur, for example, when a new DTV antenna is added to a tower, and the rules help ensure that moving the antenna does not cause new interference to other authorized stations.

ATSC DTV Considerations

ATSC (digital) pictures never display ghosts because of the way the picture is carried as digital data. As mentioned in Chapter 15, the DTV receiver is able to cancel out the unwanted echoes using circuitry called an *equalizer*, and the DTV signal contains special forward error correction codes that allow the receiver to correct for errors in the received signal. However, under extreme conditions with low signal strength and/or large echoes, the DTV receiver will no longer be able to correctly decode the picture (and/or the sound), and reception will fail.

Because DTV signals are more robust than NTSC, they are usually transmitted at a much lower power level than an equivalent NTSC transmission on the same channel. Although, for various reasons, replication may not occur exactly, the aim is usually for the DTV service to replicate the service area of the existing NTSC transmitter, and thus provide all viewers with the benefits of digital television.

CHAPTER 18

Conclusion

You made it! This tutorial is now complete. To sum up, we have learned about the major components of radio and television studios and transmitter sites, their place in the end-to-end broadcast chain, and how the equipment and systems work together to produce the broadcast signal. We have also learned about the basic principles and standards on which broadcasting is based and something of the role of the FCC in regulating the industry in the United States. We have seen that AM, FM, and TV broadcast facilities have many things in common, but that there are some major differences, particularly in the world of digital broadcasting.

This is a complex subject and there are many aspects of the theory, equipment, and systems of broadcasting that we have not covered, but what we have included should give you a good understanding of the basic engineering of a radio or television broadcast facility and of the industry in general. Technologies, of course, will continue to evolve, providing an ever-widening range of tools and techniques for making and distributing audio and video programming.

We hope you have found this book to be of interest, that you now feel more comfortable discussing broadcast engineering issues, and, in particular, that the information provided will enable you to do your job more effectively.

Further Information

If you want to explore the topic of broadcast engineering further, many sources of additional information are available. For in-depth books on the various aspects of radio and televisions engineering, we suggest you visit the online bookstores of the NAB and Focal Press at:

> www.nab.org
> www.focalpress.com

The following websites are also great sources of information on broadcast standards and rules, and they have links to other related sites that you may find useful:

> www.atsc.org
> www.smpte.org
> www.aes.org
> www.ibiquity.com
> www.fcc.gov

Index